"Hitchcock sought to break the conventions of filmmaking, something you should aspire to do when you begin production on your own film. Beyond acting as a great tool for aspiring filmmakers who want to deliver a unique horror or thriller film, author Tony Lee Moral's *Alfred Hitchcock's Moviemaking Master Class* is an entertaining book for movie buffs who want to read more about Hitchcock's thoughts on film and storytelling in general. A great starting point for Hitchcock enthusiasts who want to emulate the art of the master."
— Felix Vasquez Jr., cinema-crazed.com

"Tony Lee Moral has written a primer that's perfect for film students and others just beginning to appreciate the remarkable skills of a world-class filmmaker who came to be synonymous with suspense and dark humor."
— Robin Simons, *Crescenta Valley Weekly*

"Tony Lee Moral's *Alfred Hitchcock's Moviemaking Master Class* might be the ultimate syllabus for studying the Master of Suspense's filmography. Every facet of film is looked at through Hitchcock's methodology and is a must-have addition to the library of every writer, filmmaker, or movie buff."
— Stefan Blitz, editor-in-chief, forcesofgeek.com

"No stone is left unturned as Moral examines the master's techniques, showing how modern Hollywood continues to emulate Hitchcock on the big screen. The aspiring screenwriter can use this study to discover where he can improve in his personal journey to writing and moviemaking."
— Jason T. Carter, entertainment blogger

"There are storytellers, there are movie directors, and then there's Alfred Hitchcock, who made a career out of re-telling stories and redefining filmmaking. Tony Lee Moral's book explores everything you need to know about Hitchcock and his methodologies... and then some."
— Matthew Terry, filmmaker, teacher, contributor: microfilmmaker.com

"Uses Hitchcock's approach to filmmaking to communicate a comprehensive look at all aspects of filmmaking, from the original idea to the finished product... filmmakers can learn much from walking through Moral's book."
— Tom Farr, Tom Farr Reviews

"Tony Lee Moral has done a splendid job surveying the panoply of wit, wisdom, experience and sage advice by Hitchcock, the master storyteller, whose rich palette of willful choices made across the entire spectrum of his film work is seen in every area of moviemaking vitally important to any film/TV director who plans to effectively tell stories on the screen."
— Fred G. Thorne, writer, producer, director

"For years, film students have slogged through books 'analyzing' Hitchcock according to academic film theory: the gaze, objects of desire, blah blah blah. These books may help make great thesis papers, but they certainly don't help make BETTER MOVIES. Enter Moral's book, which not only approaches Hitchcock with a smart, analytical eye, but deconstructs his films in a way that allows filmmakers to understand his techniques and use them to improve their own work."
— Chad Gervich, author: *Small Screen, Big Picture: A Writer's Guide to the TV Business*

"For any lover of Hitchcock, it is enthralling."
— Alec McCowen, star of *Frenzy*

"Positive coverage of one of the giants of film — I was privileged to be taught by him in that craft — always with courtesy, humor, and great insight. I am indebted to him."
— Barbara Leigh-Hunt, star of *Frenzy*

"Tony Lee Moral has had a brilliant idea. Whether or not one agrees with the world's critics that *Vertigo* is the greatest film ever made, no one is going to contest the idea that Hitchcock was, among many other things, the supreme master of film technique, able perhaps better than anyone else to give the fullest possible expression on film of what he wanted to say. Who better, therefore, to turn to for enlightenment on how film ought to be done? And that is precisely what Moral does in *Alfred Hitchcock's Moviemaking Master Class.*"
— John Russell Taylor, Alfred Hitchcock's authorized biographer

"Rich with detail and packed with examples from the master storyteller, Tony Lee Moral shows how keeping things under tight control, wasting nothing, and preparing properly will elevate your film to the next level. From locations to lighting, camera moves to final cut, this really is a practical blueprint for the successful suspense film."
— Robert Grant, literary editor: SCI-FI-LONDON, author: *Writing the Science Fiction Film*

"This book is like a gift wrapped in layers of flickering celluloid, each chapter projecting precise information about how the master auteur consciously and deliberately used stories, actors, lighting, and camera angles to scare the pants off us. Read it, and then watch Hitchcock movies alone in the dark. I dare you!"
— Mary J. Schirmer, screenwriter-teacher-editor, screenplayers.net

ALFRED HITCHCOCK'S

MOVIEMAKING MASTER CLASS

*Learning About Film
from the Master Of Suspense*

TONY LEE MORAL

MICHAEL WIESE PRODUCTIONS

Published by Michael Wiese Productions
12400 Ventura Blvd. #1111
Studio City, CA 91604
(818) 379-8799, (818) 986-3408 (FAX)
mw@mwp.com
www.mwp.com

Cover design by Johnny Ink. www.johnnyink.com
Interior design by William Morosi
Printed by McNaughton & Gunn

Cover photo provided courtesy of the Hitchcock estate

Manufactured in the United States of America

Library of Congress Cataloging-in-Publication Data

Moral, Tony Lee.
  Hitchcock's moviemaking master class : learning about film from the master
of suspense / Tony Lee Moral.
      pages cm
  Includes bibliographical references.
  ISBN 978-1-61593-137-8
1. Hitchcock, Alfred, 1899-1980--Criticism and interpretation. 2. Motion pic-
tures--Production and direction. 3. Cinematography. I. Title.
  PN1998.3.H58M66 2013
  791.4302'33092--dc23

                                    2013002882

Printed on Recycled Stock

This book is dedicated to Alfred Hitchcock,
the master of suspense and storytelling.

TABLE OF CONTENTS

Chapter 3
PRE-PRODUCTION

Chapter 8
DON'T WORRY — IT'S ONLY A MOVIE 201

ACKNOWLEDGMENTS

During the course of my research on Alfred Hitchcock over the last 20 years, I've had the pleasure of interviewing many actors who have worked with the director, including Diane Baker, Lucinda Barrett, Veronica Cartwright, Doris Day, Karin Dor, Mariette Hartley, Tippi Hedren, Pat Hitchcock, Barbara Leigh-Hunt, Alec McCowen, Kim Novak, Jean Marsh, Eva Marie Saint, and Rod Taylor.

I've also had memorable conversations with Hitchcock screenwriters Jay Presson Allen, Evan Hunter, and Joseph Stefano, as well as members of the Hitchcock crew: Robert Boyle, James H. Brown, Helen Colvig, Virginia Darcy, Hilton Green, Norman Lloyd, Howard Mendelson, Harold Michelson, Ted Parvin, Rita Riggs, Marshall Schlom, Howard Smits, and Gilbert Taylor.

I thank Patricia Hitchcock O'Connell, the Alfred J. Hitchcock Trust, Taylor & Faust, and Steven Kravitz for their encouragement and for granting me permission to quote from the Alfred J. Hitchcock Trust and to publish stills and storyboards, including the cover photograph of Hitchcock.

Thank you to Peter Bogdanovich, who so generously allowed me to quote from his series of interviews with Alfred Hitchcock, including many unpublished excerpts. In addition I thank Laura Truffaut for her kind permission to quote from her father's pioneering 1962 interview with Alfred Hitchcock for his seminal book *Hitchcock*. Two other works were also invaluable in my research, *Hitchcock on Hitchcock* (1997) and *Alfred Hitchcock: Interviews* (2003), both edited by Sidney Gottlieb.

Among my reviewers, I especially thank Ewan Clark, Kriistina Hackel, Christopher Hansen, Michael Kowalski, and Bill Lansman for valuable comments for the book.

I'd especially like to thank Bob Shayne, whose comments and revisions were invaluable, especially for chapters 1 and 2 on screenwriting.

I also thank Ken Lee and Michael Wiese for their support in this project and for believing that I was the man for the job. And thank you to Barbara Hall, Kristine Krueger, and the dedicated staff at the Margaret Herrick Library, Academy of Motion Pictures Arts and Sciences, in Beverly Hills, California. Also thanks to Jennifer Bass for allowing me to publish the *Psycho* storyboards from her father's collection © The Estate of Saul Bass, and Emily Boyle for the *Saboteur* storyboards in the Robert Boyle collection, © The Estate of Robert F Boyle. The black and white stills were provided by Jerry Ohlinger Movie Stores with the permission of the Alfred J. Hitchcock Trust. The author's photograph with Brann the raven was kindly provided by Lloyd & Rose Buck and courtesy of Jo Sarsby Management.

And finally to Alfred Hitchcock, who has continually captivated my imagination with his cinematic magic.

Also by Tony Lee Moral
The Making of Hitchcock's The Birds
Hitchcock and the Making of Marnie

INTRODUCTION

Good day. My name is Alfred Hitchcock, and I will be your personal guide through the making of a motion picture....

Portrait of Alfred Hitchcock

Alfred Hitchcock was inarguably one of the greatest filmmakers of the 20th century. He was also one of the most influential directors in motion picture history, inspiring many others through his understanding of all aspects of cinema and his innovative approach to filmmaking. All of his collaborators, including screenwriters, assistant directors, actors, and production staff testify that not only was Hitchcock a first-rate *auteur*, he was also a great teacher, regularly engaging with his audiences and giving lectures at film institutes, universities, and film schools across the country. "He was a great director, who inspired many others," says Jay Presson Allen, the screenwriter of Hitchcock's *Marnie* (1964). "I couldn't learn as fast as he could teach." "He was a great entertainer," agrees Norman Lloyd, Hitch's long-time producer and friend. "People knew that with a Hitchcock picture they would have a good time, they may be frightened, they may be amused, he had this individual personality as a storyteller. Hitch had that greatest of all things, a story to tell. He will be remembered as the Master."

In a career spanning six decades, Hitchcock directed 57 feature films, 18 episodes of the television series

Alfred Hitchcock Presents and *The Alfred Hitchcock Hour* (introducing 361 total episodes), and oversaw a series of books and a mystery magazine bearing his name. He became a director at the age of 25 and pioneered many techniques in the suspense and thriller genre, framing shots to maximize anxiety and fear and using innovative film editing techniques to create shock and surprise. Although Hitchcock never won a competitive Oscar, he was nominated fives times as Best Director for *Rebecca* (1940), *Lifeboat* (1944), *Spellbound* (1945), *Rear Window* (1954), and *Psycho* (1960). He won two Golden Globes, a BAFTA Academy Fellowship award, eight Laurel Awards, and two honorary Academy Awards. In 1979, a year before he died, Hitchcock was given a lifetime achievement award by the American Film Institute. In a 2012 poll by *Sight and Sound* magazine, his masterpiece *Vertigo* (1958) was named the number one film of all time, surpassing such greats as *Citizen Kane* (1941), *Tokyo Story* (1953), and *2001: A Space Odyssey* (1968).

This book is intended for everyone with an interest in film, not just for fans of Hitchcock or film students. Anyone who enjoys film will enjoy this book if they want to know what makes a film good, because who better to teach you about film than Alfred Hitchcock? His work is an exemplary model for understanding the art and craft of film, because of his understanding of pure cinema. Not only was Hitchcock the "Master of Suspense," he was also a master of directing, framing, editing, scoring, casting, and marketing. By studying Hitchcock you study everything filmmaking encompasses.

As a filmmaker myself, with a lifelong interest in Hitchcock, the more I delve into the making of his films, the more I appreciate his artistry as a consummate craftsman who thoroughly understood the business of moviemaking. Through my two books on the making of *The Birds* and *Marnie*, I have extensively researched the Alfred J.

Hitchcock collection held at the Margaret Herrick Library in Beverly Hills, delved into his production notes, interviewed many of the key personnel who worked with Hitch, including writers, actors, art directors, costumer designers, storyboard artists, and illustrators. All of his co-workers have affirmed to me that Hitchcock was one of the most collaborative directors that they have worked with, who not only knew his job, but everyone else's on the movie set.

Although Hitchcock was the "Master" of suspense movies, his general approach to cinema applies to all types of genres, not only films that are explicitly suspenseful. Traditional films that share elements of suspense and the manipulation of information to create suspense include dramas, action adventures, and romantic comedies. This is the very paradigm that underlies good storytelling. Although you may not want to make a suspense film, it's valuable to learn how Hitchcock's cinematic practices apply to your film, no matter what type of film you do want to make, because his principles are the very foundation of filmmaking.

Take, for example, a summer blockbuster like *The Amazing Spider-Man* (2012). On the surface it doesn't seem to have much in common with Hitchcock, being an adaptation of a Marvel comic book. But if you take a closer look at the film, many of the suspense techniques, the withholding of information, the manipulation of audience identification with the central characters, the use of point of view, etc., shows just how close to the Hitchcock model it really is. Further clues can be seen in the posters of Hitchcock movies prominently displayed in the background — for example there's a poster of *Rear Window* in Peter Parker's bedroom — showing that the central characters in both films are photographers. Peter grieving for Gwen also meets a redhead played by the same actress, Emma Stone, in a scene with shades of *Vertigo*. There's even an appearance by comic book legend Stan Lee as the librarian, in the style of Hitchcock's famous cameos.

What do other movies like *The Bourne Identity* (2002), *Shutter Island* (2010), *The Ghost Writer* (2010), and *Source Code* (2011) all have in common? They too were all inspired by Hitchcock. Martin Scorsese, a longtime admirer of the director, says, "You can watch Hitchcock's films over and over throughout your life and find something new every time. There's always more to learn. And as you get older, the films change with you. After a while, you stop counting the great number of times you've seen them. I've looked at Hitchcock's films in sections. Just like the greatest music or painting, you can live with, or by, his films. And you can't say that about every director."

You don't just have to like thrillers to appreciate Hitchcock. He pioneered and revolutionized the way all kinds of stories were told on screen. Not only the way he handled suspense, but also romance and comedy. Even the most romantic love story needs suspense. As Kim Novak, who starred in his romantic epic *Vertigo* says, "Hitchcock is one of the great directors and one to be studied. He was a perfectionist. He didn't make any short cuts like some directors do today. There wasn't a part of the movie he wouldn't have a say in. When you are studying his work, you are watching the total making of a movie."

This book is intended for everyone with an appreciation of film and for those who want to make a film, whether they are a screenwriter, production designer, editor, or an aspiring director. It's also intended for fans of Hitchcock, in the hope that they can gain a deeper understanding of his methods and genius as a filmmaker. By understanding how Hitchcock, the "Master Filmmaker," conceived his films, both the novice and the more experienced student will develop in the process a deeper knowledge of how films are made and what makes a film good.

Now in this master class, we will take you through the process of making of a movie, with Alfred Hitchcock as your guide. Each chapter covers a different aspect of filmmaking, from coming up with an initial story idea through writing the full screenplay; prepping sets, costumes, storyboards, and shots; casting and directing actors; and post-production editing, scoring, and marketing. We'll be using examples from Hitchcock's films, which span the history of 20th century cinema.

Using unpublished material from both the Alfred Hitchcock Collection in Beverly Hills, as well as interviews with the "Master" himself and his long-standing collaborators, including actors, writers, and technicians, this book is an insider's guide to moviemaking. We'll discover tips from Hitchcock on how to tell a story visually rather than merely through photographs of people talking, how to compose a shot, and how to create suspense through framing, editing, and music. As Hitchcock said, "I'm not interested in content, but more in the technique of storytelling by means of film."

The master class is designed as an ongoing tool for making your own movies. The exercises at the end of each chapter are laid out to stimulate the reader and give a better appreciation of Hitchcock's cinematic techniques. They are designed to be used by the film student, in class, by individuals or groups, as a starting point for further discussion in conjunction with a recommended viewing list of Hitchcock's key films.

Although in this master class we acknowledge Alfred Hitchcock as a giant of cinema, we recognize at the same time that modern audiences are appreciative of contemporary directors such as Martin Scorsese, David Fincher, Christopher Nolan, Steven Spielberg, and Peter Jackson. All these filmmakers routinely have big budgets at their disposal, and their films are driven by action sequences, special effects and CGI, often planned using pre-visualization. So Hitchcock's methods of meticulous planning has been emulated in the thirty years since his death. There is no director whose films are taught more than Hitchcock's, and whole courses are built around him at schools and universities across the country.

Hitchcock believed that film schools should teach the history of cinema as much as anything from the beginning. "I'm a puritan and believer in the visual," said Hitchcock. "And that's what I think schools should teach. So often you hear of schools, which send out a student with an 8mm camera and see what he observes. That's only a part of it." As director and Hitchcock fan William Friedkin says, "Just watch the films of Alfred Hitchcock, that's all you need to know on how to make films."

As well as looking to the "Master" for ideas and inspiration, directors have remade and reworked his films, borrowed his themes and images, and delivered their own homages and tributes. Just one film, *Psycho*, has inspired three sequels, a shot-by-shot remake by Gus Van Sant, and an entire genre of slasher films, from *Halloween* (1978) to *Smiley* (2012). As *Halloween* director John Carpenter says, "I look at Hitchcock as a valuable natural resource since I try to steal from him as often as I possibly can. Emotionally, I grew up watching Hitchcock movies and learning cinematic technique without realizing I was actually in a filmmaking classroom rather than a movie theatre. Beyond the obvious clichés of 'Master of Suspense,' Hitchcock loved pure cinema. More than loving it, he understood it in as profound a way as any great director before or since."

At this writing, 32 years after his death and 90 years after his first directed film, Alfred Hitchcock remains as present as ever in the public consciousness, as proven by the recent feature film *Hitchcock*, starring Anthony Hopkins, guaranteed to advance even further the legacy of the moviemaking genius.

So sit back, be prepared to be thrilled and entertained on a rollercoaster ride, and let Alfred Hitchcock be your guide as we uncover the tips and techniques that made him one of the greatest film artists of the 20th century.

CHAPTER ONE

TELL ME THE STORY SO FAR

"Well, for me, it all starts with the basic material first...you may have a novel, a play, an original idea, a couple of sentences and from that the film begins." — Alfred Hitchcock

Two strangers meet on a train and plot to trade murders; a wheelchair-bound photographer passes the time by spying on his neighbors through his rear window; while vacationing abroad, an American couple become caught up in an assassination plot when their son is kidnapped; a young woman is stabbed to death in a motel shower by an unknown assailant; flocks of birds inexplicably attack a seaside town. All of these ideas have the indelible stamp of one director — Alfred Hitchcock, a master of suspense and the macabre. "I think that all the films I make are fantasies," said Hitchcock. "They are not slices of life, they are larger than life."

WRITE DOWN YOUR IDEA ON A BLANK PIECE OF PAPER

Hitchcock often started with larger than life ideas when thinking about the plot of his films and he would write down his idea on a blank piece of paper. Imagine wanting to film a scene across the faces of Mount Rushmore. Or someone addressing the general assembly of the United Nations refusing to continue until the delegate of Peru wakes up. When the delegate is tapped on the shoulder, he falls over dead. Or a fight to the finish atop the Statue of Liberty?

In finding his ideas, Hitchcock often turned to newspaper articles, short stories, plays, and novels. In Hitchcock's stories about love and romance a woman is persuaded to go to bed with a Nazi spy for the good of her country in *Notorious* (1946), and in *Vertigo* (1958), a retired detective attempts to reshape a shop girl into the image of his lost love. These are just some of the many examples where Hitchcock takes one basic idea and spins it into a movie.

The idea for *Notorious* arose from a newspaper article about a young woman in love with the son of a prominent New York socialite. The woman feared that a secret from her past — that she had slept with a foreign spy to gain valuable information — would destroy her chance of happiness. Hitchcock and his screenwriter Ben Hecht decided to keep only the part about the young woman pressed into sexual service for her country. From that idea arose the plotting for one of Hitch's finest films, which is more of a love story than a suspense story. As he said about *Notorious*, "The whole film was really designed as a love story. I wanted to make this film about a man who forces a woman to go to bed with another man because it's his professional duty. The politics of the thing didn't much interest me."

Roger Thornhill (Cary Grant) and Eve Kendall (Eva Marie Saint) are chased across the faces of Mount Rushmore (*North by Northwest*, 1959).

Vertigo was based on a French novella, *D'entre les morts* — literally translated *From Among the Dead* — about a detective, suffering from a fear of heights, who is hired to follow the troubled wife of a friend. From this idea, screenwriter Samuel Taylor came up with the San Francisco locations, the characters, and the powerful theme of obsessive love. As Taylor said, Hitchcock was "the master of the situation, the vignette, the small moment, the short story; he always knew what he wanted to do with those." These ideas were part of a mosaic, and when you put the mosaic together, then you have the whole story.

Torn Curtain (1966), about an American physicist who pretends to defect across the Iron Curtain, to the dismay of his fiancée, was conceived from real-life events. When Hitchcock read about British spies Burgess and Maclean defecting to Russia during World War II, he wondered, "What did Mrs. Maclean think of the whole thing?"

PITCHING YOUR IDEA

> *"Life is a big mystery. I think people are intrigued about mystery, to find out about things that they don't know anything about."*
> — *Alfred Hitchcock*

Hitchcock kept his stories simple so that the audience could follow them. If anything in your story is densely plotted and convoluted, you won't get the suspense out of it. Abstract stories tend to confuse the audience, which is why Hitch tended to favor crime stories with spies, assassinations, and people running from the police, which was suited to his highly visual style. Although he complained that "crime fiction is second-class literature in America" compared to Britain, where it was more highly regarded, it also gave Hitchcock some of his greatest films, including *Rope*, *Strangers on a Train*, *Rear Window*, and *Psycho*. These sorts of plots make it easier to play on fear and suspense. Can you pitch these stories in an elevator in one line?

Screenwriter Ernest Lehman was originally contracted to write a screenplay from the novel *The Wreck of the Mary Deare*, but couldn't find the inspiration to do so. Instead he said to Hitch, "I want to do the Hitchcock picture to end all Hitchcock pictures. It has to have glamour, wit, sophistication, and move all over the place with suspense." Hitch's response was, "I always wanted to do a scene on Mount Rushmore, where the hero hides in Abraham Lincoln's nose." This scene got both Lehman and Hitchcock thinking in a Northwesterly direction, but it took them almost a year to write *North by Northwest* because it was an original idea.

Hitchcock liked the first 65 pages of Lehman's script and went to the execs at MGM, who had been expecting an adaptation of *Mary Deare*. Hitch was a master storyteller and adept at selling ideas to execs, so he pitched the story premise and first 20 minutes of *North by Northwest*, not knowing where the story was going to go. The execs were thrilled — they thought they were going to get two Hitchcock movies instead of one. Then Hitchcock looked at his wristwatch and said "Well gentlemen, I have a meeting to attend. I'll see you at the preview." But he did such a good pitch that the execs at MGM were spellbound and commissioned the film on the spot. Typical Hitch!

A story should begin with a basic premise. This is your starting point and involves a protagonist who must be proactive and have a goal. In *Notorious*, a woman must pretend to be in love with a Nazi in order to obtain top-secret information. That's a story premise. You have the protagonist, her goal (obtaining information), and some idea of the major obstacle (not being found out). A pitch is the presentation of the main points of your premise in a way that convinces a producer to buy. It's usually about 500 to 2,000 words in length.

WRITE A CATCHY LOGLINE

A logline is a very brief explanation of your story — usually one to three sentences long — designed to grab the attention of a reader or producer. It contains the basic elements of the protagonist, the conflict, the antagonist, and the genre. The logline is a concise description of the movie including its essential hook. Think about these basic ideas in Hitchcock's films, and how the titles are mirrored in the following loglines.

A woman is haunted by her husband's obsessive memory of his first wife — *Rebecca*.

A wheelchair-bound photographer spying on his neighbors suspects that one of them is a murderer — *Rear Window*.

A secretary embezzles $40,000 from her employer and while on the run encounters a young motel owner under the domination of his murderous mother — *Psycho*.

A wealthy San Francisco socialite pursues a potential boyfriend to a small Northern California town that slowly takes a turn for the bizarre when birds of all kind suddenly begin to attack people with increasing viciousness — *The Birds*.

COMING UP WITH YOUR OWN IDEA — ORIGINAL SCREENPLAYS

Although Hitchcock developed only six of his movies from original screenplays — *The Ring* (1927), *Foreign Correspondent* (1940), *Saboteur* (1942), *Notorious* (1946), *North by Northwest* (1959), and *Torn Curtain* (1966) — he loved spinning ideas from his own imagination, and from the imaginations of his screenwriting collaborators.

Like Hitch, Steven Spielberg says that he "dreams for a living" and has the audience in mind when he makes a film. Quentin Tarantino sees himself as more of a writer/ director rather than a director. "The glory in what I do is that it starts with a blank piece of paper," says Tarantino. "If you look at something like *Inglourious Basterds* (2009), and if my mother had never met my father, that would never have existed in any way, shape, or form...it started with a pen and paper."

Tarantino admits that it's hard work to start from scratch. Even though you may have made many movies before, it doesn't necessarily help you. He believes that while it may be easier to direct other people's scripts and work with the screenwriter, six years down the line you may have lost your original writer's voice. Even though he loved filming the novel adaptation *Jackie Brown* (1997), Tarantino says that he doesn't want to adapt other people's work in the future, but instead wants to continue coming up with his own original ideas.

Alfred Hitchcock wasn't short of original ideas, but he most often preferred to build those ideas around solid source material.

ADAPTING SOMEONE ELSE'S IDEA — ADAPTED SCREENPLAYS

"A best-seller in literature is one thing — it doesn't necessarily mean it's going to be a best-seller in film."" — *Alfred Hitchcock*

If you don't have your own original idea you can adapt someone else's, which is what Hitchcock most often did. One of his biggest challenges was to find exciting and original source material to adapt, so he turned to short stories, novels, plays, and newspaper articles for inspiration. Some of his films from novels include *Rebecca* (1940), *Psycho* (1960), *Marnie* (1964), and *Frenzy* (1972); from plays, *Rope* (1948), *I Confess* (1953), *Dial M for Murder* (1954); from short stories or novellas, *Rear Window* (1954), *Vertigo* (1958), and *The Birds* (1963).

Hitchcock was reluctant to adapt major and popular literature, such as Fyodor Dostoevsky's *Crime and Punishment*, whose theme of guilt, murder, and redemption would seem perfect for him. In fact he often made successful films from extremely mediocre material and pulp fiction. As he said, "I have always maintained that it is supreme foolishness to take any book and film the whole of it, just because one angle of it is really worth screening." Most often in Hitchcock's adaptations he ran with the ideas from the source material that interested him most, while ignoring the source material as a whole.

When he was developing *The 39 Steps* (1935), Hitchcock saw the promise of John Buchan's original story, but couldn't see it in its entirety as good film material. So he took some of the novel's characters, part of the plot and the locations, and created the story of an innocent man on the run, accused of a crime he didn't commit and caught up in a web of international intrigue. Very often Hitchcock didn't read the entire novel or story, but just took the basic premise. For example, *The Birds* bears little resemblance to Daphne du Maurier's short story set in Cornwall, apart from the idea of birds attacking humans. As Hitch said, "It isn't because I want to change the story...I just take the basic idea. I only read the story once, and never look at it again."

Sometimes Hitchcock would write a scenario without even completing the original book, knowing only the bare plot, the characters, and the rough outline. The basic idea may be in any of these elements or in certain of the situations. But if you plan to adapt a book, be careful, because a good book doesn't necessarily mean it will make a good film. Hitchcock's *Topaz* (1969) was adapted from Leon Uris' novel, a best-seller at the time, but the result wasn't a successful movie.

THEMES IN YOUR STORY

You now have the idea for your movie, but what are the major themes and what kind of story do you want to tell? The theme is the idea behind your story, the central characteristic, concern or motif. It can be a moral, but doesn't have to be. For Hitchcock, the themes must blend two important elements.

Firstly, your theme should hang on one single central idea that the audience must always be thinking about. Hitch believed the formula for making an exciting film is to find a single problem, which is sufficiently enthralling to hold the attention of the audience while the story unfolds. A good movie formula states in the first ten minutes the film's central theme and dilemma. The theme of *Notorious* is the conflict between love and duty. It's an agent's job to push the woman he loves into a villain's bed in order to gain strategic information. The villain is a rather appealing figure, because his love for the woman is probably deeper than the agent's. All three characters are caught up not only in a spy story, but also in a psychological conflict between love and duty.

Secondly, your theme must have scope to introduce a number of other elements or sub-themes in the movie. For Hitchcock, such themes included love (*Vertigo*), guilt and innocence (*The Wrong Man*), psychology (*Marnie*), and morality (*Rope*). As Hitch understood, deep underlying themes add essential emotional resonance to the surface plot.

THE WRONGFULLY ACCUSED MAN

"I'm not against the police, I'm just afraid of them. " — Alfred Hitchcock

The "wrongfully accused man" was a subject Hitchcock returned to repeatedly throughout his career in stories often featuring innocent men forced to dodge both the real villains and the police until they can unmask the true criminal and prove their innocence. *The 39 Steps* (1935), *Saboteur* (1942), *The Wrong Man* (1956), *North by Northwest* (1959), and *Frenzy* (1972) all revolved around mistaken identities and wrongful accusations.

One reason behind Hitchcock's fondness for the wrongfully accused man story is a structural one. The audience must have sympathy for the man on the run. But they will wonder, "Why doesn't he go to the police?" Well, the police are after him, so he can't go to them. Otherwise

The innocent Manny Balestrero (Henry Fonda) lines up in *The Wrong Man* (1956).

there will be no chase story. The important thing is that he cannot and must not go to the police. Hitchcock stated that his greatest fear was of the police, and he often told the story of when he was five years old his father sent him to the local police station, "with a note to the chief of police, who read the note and promptly put me into a cell and locked the door for five minutes; and then let me out, saying, 'That's what we do to naughty little boys.'"

The man on the run in these wrongfully accused films is the average man. He's not a professional, detective, or criminal, but the everyman. As Hitchcock said, "That helps involve the audience much more easily than if he was unique. I have never been interested in making films about professional criminals or detectives. I much prefer to take average men, because I think the audience can get involved more easily." So for Hitchcock, the theme of the innocent, wrongfully accused man taps into the audience's own fear that it could easily be them in the same position.

In Hitchcock's films, the best example of the wrongfully accused man is *The Wrong Man*, the true story of musician Manny Balestrero (played by Henry Fonda) who was falsely accused of armed robbery. As Hitchcock said, "Well it happens so often, and I think it creates a rooting interest within an audience, because nobody likes to be accused of something that he wasn't responsible for." *The Wrong Man* being a true story added to the audience fascination.

Martin Scorsese, when making his New York-based movie *Taxi Driver* (1976), was inspired by Hitchcock's film. "*The Wrong Man* is a picture I often used repeatedly for mood, paranoid style, beautiful New York location photography," says Scorsese. "And I think ultimately it's the reason I asked [Hitchcock composer] Bernard Herrmann to do the score. I think about the paranoid camera moves, the feelings of threat when Henry Fonda goes to pay his insurance in Queens. He's standing behind the counter and the woman's looking over and you see Henry Fonda from this point of view. And the way the camera moves, her perception, excellent bit part players, the fear, the anxiety and the paranoia, is all done through the camera and the performer's face."

This theme of the wrongfully accused man is a popular one in today's movies, from *The Fugitive* (1993), *The Shawshank Redemption* (1994), and *Minority Report* (2002), to *Eagle Eye* (2008) and *The Adjustment Bureau* (2011).

THE DUPLICITOUS BLONDE

"Blondes make the best victims — they're like virgin snow that shows up the bloody footprints."— Alfred Hitchcock

Hitchcock is famous for casting blonde leading ladies who are cool, mysterious, and elegant. Throughout his career he gave us some of the screen's most fascinating, complex, and duplicitous female characters. Memorable "Hitchcock blondes" include Madeleine Carroll in *The 39 Steps* and *Secret Agent*, Joan Fontaine in *Rebecca* and *Suspicion*, Ingrid Bergman in *Spellbound*, *Notorious*, and *Under Capricorn*, Grace Kelly in *Dial M for Murder*, *Rear Window*, and *To Catch a Thief*, Kim Novak in *Vertigo*, Eva Marie Saint in *North by Northwest*, and Tippi Hedren in *The Birds* and *Marnie*.

These women are often punished for a crime that they have committed, such as the characters played by Janet Leigh in *Psycho*, Kim Novak in *Vertigo*, and Tippi Hedren in *Marnie*. Ever since his early film *The Lodger* (1927), where the serial killer, a Jack the Ripper type, murders

The morally conflicted Alicia Huberman (Ingrid Bergman) in *Notorious* (1946).

blonde women, Hitchcock maintained that blondes make the best victims. He loved contrast, so he presented women who were very ladylike on the surface. As Tippi Hedren said, "He liked to take women of strength who are pretty much together, put them in a situation and jumble them around and see how they come out." In *The 39 Steps*, the public sees that Madeleine Carroll has no time to be her usual sophisticated self — she is far too busy racing over moors, rushing up and down embankments, and scrambling over rocks.

Today's blonde femme fatales have been inspired by Hitchcock heroines. Think of Glenn Close in *Fatal Attraction* (1987), Sharon Stone in *Basic Instinct* (1992), Kim Basinger in *L.A. Confidential* (1997), and Naomi Watts in *Mulholland Dr.* (2001).

THE PSYCHOPATH

"I'd like to discuss a subject very dear to me — homicide." — *Alfred Hitchcock*

The serial killer or psychopath has long fascinated Hitchcock ever since *The Lodger* (1927). His films feature a roster of crazy psychopaths. In Hitch's favorite of his films, *Shadow of a Doubt* (1943), a beloved uncle is really the "Merry Widow Murderer." In *Rope* (1948), two buttoned-down students are actually thrill killers. Two men swap murders in *Strangers on a Train* (1951). In *Psycho* (1960), motel manager Norman Bates has guest (and mommy) issues, and in *Frenzy* (1972), a rapist and murderer leaves a necktie around the neck of each of his victims.

What do these crazy guys have in common? They are all attractive and seductive. As Hitchcock knew too well, evil is attractive, otherwise the murderers would never be able to get near to their victims. We'll be getting up close to these villains too in more detail in Chapter 4 to show

Anthony Perkins as the psychopathic boy next door, Norman Bates, in *Psycho* (1960).

how Hitchcock cast and directed actors, often against type, to play these sympathetic murderers.

The attractive psychopath is a tradition that continues in recent movies. The characters played by Robert De Niro in *Cape Fear* (1991), Anthony Hopkins in *The Silence of the Lambs* (1991), Matt Damon in *The Talented Mr. Ripley* (1999), and Stanley Tucci in *The Lovely Bones* (2009) all owe a debt to Hitchcock. All of these murderers are charming, devious, sympathetic, and deadly.

SECRETS AND SPIES

The spy genre is one of the oldest in film history and Hitchcock was fascinated with spies and secrets. Many of his films deal in espionage, such as *Secret Agent, The 39 Steps, Sabotage, Saboteur, Foreign Correspondent, The Man Who Knew Too Much, North by Northwest,*

Torn Curtain, and *Topaz*. Hitchcock spies are either ordinary men plunged into the world of espionage, such as James Stewart's American doctor abroad in *The Man Who Knew Too Much* (1956) or Cary Grant's advertising exec in *North by Northwest* (1959). Or they are real spies, as in *Secret Agent* (1936) and *Topaz* (1969). As Hitchcock remarked, spies are really two different people — heroes in their own country and villains in the foreign country. This contrast fascinated him.

These early spy films from Hitchcock heralded the way for today's iconic spy characters, as *North by Northwest* (1959) triggered the cycle of James Bond films. Indeed the attack on Bond by the helicopter in *From Russia with Love* (1963) bears many similarities to Cary Grant being pursued by the crop-duster plane, as do chase sequences in *The Prize* (1963) and *Arabesque* (1966). But by the mid 1960s, Hitchcock had tired of that character, feeling that the Bond films had become a "comic book" version of his original idea, so he set out to make more realistic spy thrillers such as *Torn Curtain* (1966) and *Topaz* (1969). In recent years, Hitchcock's spy films have heavily influenced both the *Bourne* and *Mission: Impossible* series.

CONTENT

"So many people are interested in the content, that if you painted a still life of some apples on a plate, you'd be worrying whether the apples are sweet or sour. Who cares? I don't care myself." — Alfred Hitchcock

You've decided on the theme for your movie, now you need to inject a heavy dose of content and bring your movie to life. Hitchcock famously declared that he didn't care about content in his movies, and that he was more interested in film technique. As long as the audience reacted in a certain way, the idea for the film could be about anything you like. "If you begin to worry about the details, about the papers. I don't care what the spies are after," Hitchcock said. First and foremost he put cinematic style before content; "I don't even know who was in that airplane attacking Cary Grant. I don't care. So long as that audience goes through that emotion."

What did Hitch mean by these quotes? Does that mean that you shouldn't care about the content of your movies too? As Jim Brown, his assistant director on *The Birds* and *Marnie* said, Hitchcock often said things in public that were intended to shock or otherwise create reaction and controversy, not to be taken literally. What he really meant was that "It's not the story, it's what you do with it, it's the how. I find that with many people they look at a film and they look at its content only, and never seem to study what it was in the film that made an audience go through the various emotions you've put them through, especially in my field, which is thrill and suspense."

Although Hitchcock may have said he doesn't care about content, it's the content that creates suspense. In order to achieve this, one of the necessary ingredients of the formula is a series of plausible situations with people that are real. When characters are unbelievable, you never get real suspense, only surprise. It may not matter who the pilot flying the crop duster is, but it does matter that someone with a motive (content) has hired them to kill our hero. There must be motivation to make us care, and what Hitchcock is the master at is keeping the audience emotionally involved. That's the definition of suspense — content.

This all leads naturally into what Hitchcock called the "MacGuffin" — a key plot device in his films that drives the story.

THE MACGUFFIN — WHAT IS IT? (AND DOES IT MATTER?)

"It's the device, the gimmick."
— Alfred Hitchcock

Hitchcock often talked about "the MacGuffin" in his films, but what exactly is it? Let's hear it in Hitch's own words: "It might be a Scottish name, taken from a story about two men in a train. One man says, 'What's that package up there in the baggage rack?' and the other answers, 'Oh, that's a MacGuffin.' The first one asks, 'What's a MacGuffin?' 'Well,' the other man says, 'It's an apparatus for trapping lions in the Scottish Highlands.' The first man says 'But there are no lions in the Scottish Highlands,' and the other one answers, 'Well, then that's no MacGuffin!' So you see, a MacGuffin is nothing at all."

Cary Grant, Eva Marie Saint, Alfred Hitchcock and James Mason ponder the MacGuffin, in this case microfilm hidden inside a ceramic statue, during the filming of *North by Northwest* (1959).

Does it make any sense? Or are you still in the dark? Well that's half the point. The MacGuffin is the engine of the story and was coined by Hitchcock scenario editor Angus McPhail. It is the object around which the plot revolves, and motivates the actions of the characters. It could be stealing the secret papers, the plans to a fort, an airplane engine, or an atomic bomb, and is the thing that everyone in the film wants, but the audience doesn't really care about.

Often a MacGuffin is central to thrillers, spy stories, and adventures, and becomes very important in a Hitchcock movie. Most of the characters in the story will base their actions on the MacGuffin, although the final result will usually be of greater significance than actually getting, controlling, or destroying the MacGuffin. So a MacGuffin's purpose is to motivate the characters into action.

Examples of the MacGuffin in Hitchcock's films.

The 39 Steps — Top secret plans for a revolutionary aircraft engine.

Notorious — Radioactive uranium ore.

North by Northwest — Government secrets hidden on microfilm inside a pre-Colombian ceramic statue. Hitchcock called it "my best MacGuffin" — the emptiest, the most nonexistent, and the most absurd.

Psycho — $40,000 in stolen cash.

The Birds — The reason why the birds attack.

Torn Curtain — The secret formula for an anti-missile device.

Family Plot — Valuable diamonds.

Hitchcock was joking when he told his story about the lions in the Scottish highlands. But if the MacGuffin is important to your characters, it has to be important to your audience. They've got to know and understand enough to become emotionally involved. When Hitch and his screenwriter Ben Hecht were writing *Notorious*, the MacGuffin of the uranium ore became so involved it actually got in the way of the real plot, which was about a woman, played by Ingrid Bergman, who has to go to bed with a Nazi sympathizer. She chooses duty over love, as does her real lover, played by Cary Grant. (When researching *Notorious*, Hitchcock quite coincidentally asked a Caltech scientist how big an atomic bomb was, and he later heard that the FBI kept him under surveillance for three months!)

In *North by Northwest*, the MacGuffin is the narrative device that propels the plot, but who in the audience really cares about the roll of microfilm in the pre-Colombian statue? They're having too much fun watching Cary Grant run all over the map and fall in love with Eva Marie Saint. As Hitchcock said, "A true MacGuffin will get you where you need to go, but never overshadow what is ultimately there."

For the first 40 minutes of *Psycho*, the audience becomes invested in the character of Marion Crane (Janet Leigh), who flees town after having stolen $40,000 in cash from her boss. But then she is suddenly killed in a motel room shower, and the cash is casually tossed along with her body into the trunk of her car, which itself ends up in a swamp. The film's real story then begins, which is about who killed Marion and why. The MacGuffin — the money — got Marion to that shower, and that's all that really matters.

Examples of the MacGuffin in other directors' films.

During an interview for *Star Wars* (1977), George Lucas described R2D2 as "The MacGuffin...the main driving force of the movie, or the central object of every character's search." That's because both the Rebels and the Empire were after the plans of the Death Star inside R2D2, and the search for R2D2 drove the plot of that film.

In Quentin Tarantino's *Pulp Fiction* (1994), the viewer never finds out what's inside the briefcase, which bookends the movie. All that matters is that this MacGuffin is wanted by a crime boss, who sends his two thugs, played by Samuel L. Jackson and John Travolta, to retrieve it.

In *Avatar* (2009), the MacGuffin is the "Unobtanium," the sought-after mineral that sets the plot in motion (much like the uranium in Hitchcock's *Notorious*) — ultimately inconsequential to the actual story being told.

KEEP YOUR PLOT MOVING

"When making a picture, my ambition is to present a story that never stands still."
— *Alfred Hitchcock*

"The length of the film should be directly related to the endurance of the human bladder." — *Alfred Hitchcock*

You have your MacGuffin and all of your characters are after it, and now it's on to the chase. Hitchcock used to say that there should be a slogan, "Keep them awake at the movies!" As he well knew, films usually play from 90 to 130 minutes, and an audience starts to tire after an hour, and so they need an injection of what he called "dope." The "dope" to keep them awake is action, movement, and excitement. But there is more to it than that, because movies need careful pacing, fast action, and quick editing. A well-paced film should keep the audience's mind occupied and this is achieved not necessarily by acting or quick editing, but by a very full story and the changing of one situation to another. "Sequences can never stand still, they must carry the action forward, just as the wheels of a ratchet mountain railway move the train up the slope, cog by cog," said Hitch. "A film cannot be compared to a play or a novel. It is closer to a short story, which, as a rule, sustains one idea that culminates when the action has reached the highest point of the dramatic curve."

Hitchcock never filmed a physical chase just for the sake of it. For every film, your central character should have a goal, an aim, and the audience should be rooting for that character. A chase is essentially someone running toward a goal, or fleeing from a pursuer (which is actually the pursuer running toward a goal). Hitchcock said, "Probably the fox hunt would be the simplest form of the chase." But put in place a girl instead of the fox, and substitute the boy for the hunters, then you have a chase of boy after girl, or the police chasing a criminal. So long as a plot has either flight or pursuit, it may be considered a form of the chase. In many ways the chase — whether in low or high gear — makes up 60% of the construction of all movie plots. "Well for one thing, the chase seems to be the final expression of the motion picture medium. Where but on screen can automobiles be shown careening around corners after each other? Then too, the movie is the natural vessel for the chase story because the basic film shape is continuous. Once a movie starts it goes on."

The 39 Steps is one of Hitchcock's favorite films because of the rapid and sudden switches in location. Once the train leaves the station the film never stops moving. Such movement takes time to plan out, especially to blend the characterization with the action. Halfway through the movie, lead character Hannay (Robert Donat) leaps out of a police station window with half a handcuff on, and immediately walks into a marching Salvation Army band. To escape the police, he marches with the band, then slips into a public hall, where he's immediately mistaken for a guest speaker and ends up on an oratory platform. It's the rapid movement from one scene to another, and using one idea after another, that keeps the audience hooked.

SUSPENSE VS. MELODRAMA

"It's been my good fortune to have something of a monopoly on the genre. Nobody else seems to have taken much interest in the rules for suspense." — *Alfred Hitchcock*

Hitchcock was dubbed the "Master of Suspense" and rightly so. But what is suspense? It could be described as the stretching out of anticipation. And what is the difference between mystery and suspense? The two terms often get confused. So let's hear it from the "Master" himself: "Mystery is an intellectual process, as in [solving] a 'whodunit'...but suspense is essentially an emotional process. With suspense it's necessary to involve emotion."

One example of mystery occurs in *Vertigo* when Scottie (James Stewart) follows Madeleine (Kim Novak) to the McKittrick Hotel. He sees her in the bedroom window, but when he goes up to her room, she has disappeared, as has her car parked outside. Kim Novak remembers, "I asked Hitchcock how did Madeleine leave the hotel, because we never see her leave. His answer was 'That's why it's a mystery, my dear.' In a mystery, you don't need the answer to every question." And that was very important to Hitchcock, to leave some questions unresolved so that the audience will be thinking about them at the end of the movie.

Suspense, however, is different from mystery. Nearly all stories can do with suspense, no matter the genre. Even a love story can have suspense. It's much more than saving someone from the path of an oncoming train; there's also the suspense of whether the man will get the girl. Suspense has largely to do with the audience's own desires or wishes. So getting the suspense right in your movie is a very important part of the process. Hitchcock created different ways of generating suspense, from building story tension to editing techniques, to using sound and music to evoke terror and anticipation.

GIVE YOUR AUDIENCE INFORMATION

"There is no terror in the bang, only in the anticipation of it." — Alfred Hitchcock

All suspense comes out of giving the audience information. If you tell the audience that there's a bomb in the room and that it's going to go off in five minutes — that's suspense. Hitchcock knew how to mix the ingredients of suspense so that emotional tension became almost unbearable.

"We're sitting here talking," said Hitch in an interview, "and we don't know that there's a bomb hidden inside your tape recorder. The public doesn't know either, and suddenly the bomb explodes. We're blown to bits. Surprise. But how long does it last, the surprise and the horror? Five seconds, no more." The secret, Hitch maintained, was to let the audience in on the secret — the ticking bomb. In that way, instead of five seconds of surprise, you've created five minutes of suspense. The bomb need not even go off for the audience to have had a thrilling emotional experience.

The number one rule with suspense, then, is that you must give the audience information. For example, if something is about to harm the characters, show it at the beginning of the scene and let it play out. Constant reminders of this looming danger will build suspense and keep the audience on the edge. But remember that suspense is not in the mind of the character. They must be completely unaware of it.

A good example of this type of suspense building, where the audience knows more than the characters, occurs in *The Birds*. Melanie Daniels (Tippi Hedren) sits in front of a jungle gym outside Bodega Bay School and starts to smoke a cigarette. Unbeknownst to her, one crow lands on the bars of the jungle gym behind her. As she continues smoking obliviously, two, three, four more crows gather on the jungle gym. Finally Melanie notices a single crow in the sky and follows its movement down to the jungle gym. It is now covered in a mass of menacing crows, all awaiting Melanie's next move. The suspense in this scene is so exciting because it comes from the audience knowing more than the character. There will be more about this celebrated sequence in Chapter 6 on editing.

In *The Man Who Knew Too Much*, Hitchcock lets the audience know the moment an assassination attempt is to be made at an Albert Hall diplomatic concert — at the strike of an orchestra's cymbals. By pre-familiarizing the film's audience with the piece of music, and cutting repeatedly to the percussionist holding the cymbals, the build-up to the possible moment of murder becomes filled with suspense.

INVOLVE YOUR AUDIENCE IN THE SUSPENSE

Hitchcock made the bold decision in *Vertigo* to reveal to the audience — 40 minutes before the end of the movie — that Madeleine Elster and her mysterious doppelgänger Judy Barton (both played by Kim Novak) are in fact the same woman. Hitch said to his screenwriter Samuel Taylor, "This is the time for us to blow the whole truth." Taylor was shocked, saying, "Good God, why?" The Paramount studio executives were also against this, because they wanted the ending to be a surprise, but Hitch knew that it would be more powerful if he let the audience in on the secret.

One of the fatal things in suspense is to confuse the audience. Without knowing that Madeleine and Judy are the same person, audiences would be as confused and frustrated as Jimmy Stewart's character, Scottie. So Hitchcock decided to tell all in a flashback, and, in doing so, the audience then sits through the remaining 40 minutes of the film thinking, "What will Scottie do when he finds out that it's the same woman? What will Judy do when he finds out?" If the reveal were left to the very end, all the audience gets is five minutes of surprise. Good suspense should actively involve the audience in the telling of the story.

"I said if we don't let them know, they will speculate, some of them will even say, maybe it's the same girl," Hitchcock said. "Now they will get a blurred impression of what is going on."

In *Psycho* the audience also knows more than the characters know when detective Arbogast (Martin Balsam) enters the Bates house to investigate, one of the most suspenseful scenes in Hitchcock's films. We can't help but feel anxious for Arbogast as we know that the murderous Mrs. Bates is waiting for him at the top of the stairs. (And yet, unlike *Vertigo*'s big reveal, *Psycho*'s secret — the true identity of Mrs. Bates — is left as a final shock for both the characters and the audience. An interesting — and successful — choice on Hitchcock's part.)

Another good example of suspense building occurs in *Marnie*. The audience knows that a cleaning woman is around the corner while Marnie is robbing the Rutland office safe. Marnie doesn't know — which is more suspenseful for us, because although she's a thief, we don't want her to be caught. The irony here is that through this suspense technique the audience builds a sympathetic attachment to the wrong-doer — a Hitchcock specialty. We know that stealing is wrong, but our desire to warn Marnie about that cleaning lady ends up overwhelming our logic.

OTHER DIRECTORS USING SUSPENSE

"Suspense is like a woman. The more left to the imagination, the more the excitement."
— *Alfred Hitchcock*

Although many people think of Hitchcock's films as violent, Hitchcock actually rarely used graphic violence. Suggestion was enough in his masterful hands. In *Psycho*, after the shower scene and Arbogast's murder (themselves suggested more than graphically shown), there is less and less violence as the movie goes on. Hitch felt that he had already worked the audience into enough of an emotional state that just the expectation of possible violence was now all that was needed. Nearly all suspense movie directors draw upon the techniques used by and usually first developed by Hitchcock. One that comes to mind more than any other is Steven Spielberg. During the filming of *Jaws* (1975), Spielberg had a great deal of trouble with making the mechanical shark look authentic and frightening. Suddenly Spielberg was faced with the dilemma of having to tell a story like Hitchcock, which is that you don't show the shark for most of the movie. So he employed suspense techniques to tell the story. You see the reactions of people to the shark, you see the shark towing things through the water, you see spurting blood, you see people being yanked underwater, but you never see the shark itself, and that's something Hitchcock would have done and indeed did do during the bird attack on the Brenner house towards the end of *The Birds*. It's all filmed with suggestion.

"The whole technique which we used on *The Blair Witch Project*," says director Daniel Myrick, "and what I continue to use to this day because it's like Horror 101, and it comes from the Hitchcock Book — you give clues to what's happening or you hear what's happening or you catch glimpses of what's happening, but you don't actually see it."

Hitchcock's influence on suspense can also be clearly seen in Jonathan Demme's *The Silence of the Lambs* (1991). Demme's editor Craig McKay says, "Suspense is really an expression of fear. We can build that in our storytelling by withholding information. Frankly, it's manipulation, but in using that manipulation it also empowers the story. Not knowing where we're going to go next is the thing that human beings hate the most. We would all like to know where we're going, if it's all going to be alright." McKay and Demme always attempted to keep the audience from getting ahead of the story in *The Silence of the Lambs*, to keep it suspenseful.

Alejandro Amenábar, director of *The Others* (2001), says, "Steven Spielberg, Alfred Hitchcock, and Stanley Kubrick are the three directors that, when I was a teenager, I used to analyze their movies and watch them over and over. Their perspective — I identified with them. In the case of Hitchcock, his use of suspense is something mathematical, and my first three films — *Tesis*, *Open Your Eyes*, and *The Others* — have something to do with that."

The Bourne Identity (2002) has more action than most Hitchcock movies and also has lots of suspense and surprise together with an active chase sequence. Watch how the story is told visually, through the editing, and how the main character's point of view is used to make the audience feel like a participant in the movie. Notice how the audience often knows more about the dangers than the characters, and listen to how the tempo and type of music raises the suspense. There will be more about all of these techniques for developing suspense in the following chapters.

Many of today's movies take little time to build suspense and are often just one big explosion or CGI effect after another. You've got to give your audience time to become emotionally involved in a scene, and to build up suspense gradually, as evidenced in the crop-duster scene of *North by Northwest*. Today, you'd have the guy get off the bus, and immediately the plane would show up and chase him into the field. There would be dozens of special effects shots, and the sequence wouldn't play nearly as well emotionally with an audience. It's to Hitch's credit that he builds suspense over eight minutes of silence.

EXERCISES

1. Write down some ideas for a thriller or suspense movie and see where it leads you. What are your themes and how do they relate to the plot? Can you say what your movie is about in one sentence?

2. Lay down your story in its barest form and start to write down your idea on one piece of paper. You don't have to write very much, maybe just a man is asked to meet someone at Grand Central Station and then something eventful happens. Where does the story lead?

3. Once you've written down your idea on one sheet of paper, pitch to your friends what the film is about or try it on someone who you happen to find yourself in an elevator with for the time it takes to get from the parking garage to the floor of their office. Are you excited telling your story? Are your friends or elevator companion excited about it and want to know where your story leads?

4. Think about the protagonist for your film. Is he or she a hero or a heroine, a wrongfully accused man, a spy or a villain? Give your character attributes so that they come alive on paper.

5. Come up with an idea for a MacGuffin and how it might drive the plot in your film. Why do your characters want it so badly? Watch the following

films: *Casablanca*, *The Maltese Falcon*, and *Mission: Impossible III*. Can you spot what the MacGuffin is in these movies? How does it drive the plot?

6. Write a suspenseful scene. Make sure that the audience knows more than your characters. How does that make the scene more suspenseful?

7. Examine the ways information was manipulated in the last film you watched or in your favorite film. Focus on the first 15 minutes of the film. How are Hitchcock's cinematic practices applied to these films?

Key Hitchcock films to watch

Notorious (1946)
North by Northwest (1959)
Psycho (1960)
The Birds (1963)

Other directors' films to watch

Pulp Fiction (1994)
The Usual Suspects (1995)
Se7en (1995)
Inglourious Basterds (2009)
The Tourist (2010)

Further reading

Save the Cat! (2005) by Blake Snyder
Writing with Hitchcock (2011) by Steven De Rosa

CHAPTER TWO

WRITING YOUR SCREENPLAY

" Very often the director is no better than his script. " — Alfred Hitchcock

You have your idea for a movie, you've worked out your themes and written it down on one sheet of paper. Now it's time for the hard work — the writing of the screenplay. Hitchcock famously said that the three most vital elements of a film are "the script, the script, the script." He worked closely with his writers to construct the film, from the very beginning, on paper. Rarely would he take any writing credit himself, but guided his writers closely through every draft, paying attention to detail, with a preference toward telling the story through visual rather than verbal means.

For Hitchcock the most enjoyable part of making a movie was being in his office with his writer, discussing the storylines and deciding what they were going to put on the screen. He didn't allow the writer to go

Hitchcock at work in his study with his wife Alma, his trusted confidante.

off and just write a script that he would later interpret — he stayed involved, and included the writer in directing choices. Hitchcock's preferred writing collaborators were playwrights, novelists, screenwriters, and short story writers. And he worked with some of the best in the business, including Ben Hecht (*Spellbound, Notorious*), Thornton Wilder (*Shadow of a Doubt*), John Steinbeck (*Lifeboat*), Arthur Laurents (*Rope*), John Michael Hayes (*Rear Window, To Catch a Thief, The Man Who Knew Too Much, The Trouble With Harry*), Maxwell Anderson (*The Wrong Man*), Samuel Taylor (*Vertigo, Topaz*), Ernest Lehman (*North by Northwest, Family Plot*), and Jay Presson Allen (*Marnie*).

Usually the writing of a Hitchcock movie was a two-month job and a highly important stage to which a full understanding of the general plan was essential to the writer involved. But on *North by Northwest* (1959), because it was an original screenplay, screenwriter Ernest Lehman was in the office with Hitchcock for almost a year, and was with him on every shot and every scene. Because they started with the idea of two action and suspense scenes — a murder at the United Nations and a chase across Mount Rushmore — they had no idea of a story premise going in, unlike, for example, *Notorious*. In fact Hitchcock borrowed the basic story from *The 39 Steps* (1935) and would later call *North by Northwest* an American version of his earlier film. Hitchcock would let Lehman write the drafts, but was with him every step of the way as they shaped the initial idea into a 200-page script.

THE THREE STAGES OF THE SCREENPLAY

> *" Construction to me, it's like music. You start with your allegro, your andante, and you build up. "* — **Alfred Hitchcock**

When describing the writing of a screenplay for the *Encyclopedia Britannica*, Hitchcock outlined three stages of development, which have now become the industry standard — the outline, the treatment, and the screenplay.

THE OUTLINE

The outline gives the essence of a movie's action or story and is usually about 10 pages long. It's a scene-by-scene telling of the plot, without dialogue or description, written from the basis of the pitch. When working from source material, Hitchcock would often ask his writer to write an outline, and then work solely from that.

Screenwriter John Michael Hayes was asked to write an outline based on the short story "It Had to Be Murder" by Cornell Woolrich, which became the film *Rear Window*. When writing *Vertigo*, Samuel Taylor wrote the screenplay from Hitchcock's outline, having never read the original novella on which the outline was based. Often Hitchcock read the source material only once — for example, Robert Bloch's novel *Psycho* — and then put it aside and asked Joseph Stefano to write an outline of the story. If all the elements and characters were there, Hitchcock and his screenwriter would begin with Scene 1 in purely cinematic, rather then literary, terms.

Hitchcock said that he never approached a screenplay picturing filling a page with words, but rather filling a screen with images — a huge, white, rectangular movie theatre screen. From those images would then come words.

THE TREATMENT

Once an outline is written, the treatment is built. This is a prose version of the plot, told as if it were a short story and written in the present tense. It's a description of what appears on the screen and should be both readable and get across your story points in a voice that conveys the feeling of your movie, still without character dialogue. The hard part is that it has to get across the story, scene by scene, all the way through, with no breaks.

The whole shape of the film is roughly sketched in the treatment from the beginning, which includes the characterizations, the narrative, and even the detail, until there are about 10 to 30 pages of complete narrative. Try to avoid having anything that is not really visual in your treatment. There should be no dialogue or descriptions of any kind — no "he wondered," because you can't photograph "he wondered." As Hitchcock described it, "It's as though you were looking at the film on the screen and the sound was turned off." This is the first stage. And there's a good reason for not having any dialogue in your treatment — it's to urge yourself to make your work purely visual and to not have to rely on words to tell the story.

The treatment, then, is very full and practically the complete film on paper, in terms of action and movement. The whole movie is described for the production designers as well. When Hitchcock wrote *The 39 Steps,* he wrote a long treatment for his design team recounting the action and how the story would be visually told. He called it "making the film on paper."

As soon as the plan of the first sequence is written out, Hitchcock showed and explained it to his screenwriter so that he could feel exactly the mood of the speech required. When the treatment is on paper and the dialogue added, the whole script is then divided up into individual shots.

When Hitchcock moved to America he abandoned writing the treatment in favor of verbally describing it to his writer, and then making the corrections and adjustments afterwards. He found that the American writers wouldn't go for writing long treatments. And you may be thinking what's the point of all this pre-work, why not get on with just writing the screenplay itself? But just like Hitchcock was so meticulous, in writing the treatment you iron out all your plot points and character arcs, so by the time you sit down to write your screenplay, you've already done the hard work and you can enjoy the process of writing.

THE SCREENPLAY

The treatment is then broken down into screenplay form, which sets out the dialogue, and describes the movements and reactions of the characters. At the same time, it gives the breakdown of the individual scenes, with some indication of the role in each scene of the camera and the sound. It likewise serves as a guide to the various departments: to the art department for the sets, to the casting department for the actors, to the costume department, to makeup, to the music.

When writing *North by Northwest*, screenwriter Ernest Lehman used 3" x 5" cards and wrote each scene on one of them. He tacked them on the wall and stepped back to look at the whole movie. Sometimes he would take a card and say, "Wait a minute, this scene would be better over here." He moved the cards around as a way of getting a visual look at the film when it hadn't been shot yet.

BREAKING YOUR SCREENPLAY INTO THREE ACTS

As building the screenplay was Hitchcock's favorite part in the filmmaking process, he was obviously very concerned about structure and narrative. His films follow the conventional three-act structure in stories as diverse in plot as *Shadow of a Doubt, Strangers on a Train, Vertigo, North by Northwest, Psycho,* and *The Birds.*

In the first act, it's setting up who the characters are and what the situation of the whole story is. The second act is the progression of that situation to a high point of conflict. And the third act is how the conflicts and problems are resolved. The third act has the highest point of conflict, just before the resolution, and it builds to a climax that is bigger emotionally than anything that has happened in the second act.

In a two-hour movie, the second act is twice as long as the other two acts, and it breaks in the middle with a high or low point. So you could call it four acts if you want. Similarly, there are usually eight primary sequences in a feature film of which the first two are in Act One, the second four in Act Two, and the last two in Act Three. Each new action that moves the story forward is called a "beat," and every scene should contain at least one beat that moves the action forward. If it doesn't, Hitchcock called these scenes "non-scenes" and tended to get rid of them. The following example of 15 story beats for *North by Northwest* owes a debt to Blake Snyder's essential book on screenwriting, *Save the Cat!*:

Story beats for *North by Northwest*.

1. Opening Image (1):

Fast-talking Madison Avenue advertising exec Roger Thornhill (Cary Grant) steps out of the elevator with his secretary dictating notes along the way.

2. Theme Stated (3-5):

Thornhill is a slick city type with a mother, a secretary, two ex wives, and several bartenders dependent upon him. He is unwilling to commit to anyone and is selfish and not above dishonesty, as exhibited by his cheating another man out of a taxi by claiming that his secretary is pregnant.

3. Set-Up (1-10):

Thornhill goes to the Plaza Hotel to meet some colleagues. He's an urbanite, accustomed to plush cocktail bars and ordering martinis at the bar.

4. Catalyst/Inciting Incident (somewhere between 1 and 15):

When Thornhill goes to answer a telephone call, he is mistaken for a spy, George Kaplan, and is kidnapped by two heavies who take him at gunpoint to a mansion on Long Island.

4a. Act One Development/Complication (15)

At the mansion, Thornhill meets debonair villain Phillip Vandamm (James Mason), who's convinced that Thornhill is the spy George Kaplan and tries to kill him in a liquor-fueled car crash.

5. Debate (15-25):

After narrowly avoiding being killed, Thornill is arrested by the police for drunk driving. He is bailed out by his mother, whom he has to convince that he was truly kidnapped and returns to the Long Island Mansion with her in tow. The housekeeper there denies all knowledge of his being kidnapped and says he left the house drunk after a party.

6. Act One Turning Point/Break into Two (25-30)

A photograph in the mansion leads Thornhill to the United Nations building to seek out the house's owner, Mr. Townsend. Thornhill finds Townsend, who's suddenly knifed in the back by one of Vandamm's thugs and Thornhill is accused of killing him and has to go on the run.

7. B Story (31-35): Act Two

At Grand Central Station, Thornhill meets sexy double agent Eve Kendall (Eva Marie Saint), about to board the 20th Century Limited train for Chicago. The Professor (Leo G. Carroll), a spymaster who is after Vandamm, explains to his colleagues that they created a decoy spy named George Kaplan to protect the real spy in Vandamm's camp, and that Thornhill has been mistaken for Kaplan, who doesn't actually exist.

8. Fun and Games (35-60)

Thornhill starts a romance with Eve. When the train arrives in Chicago, Eve arranges for Thornhill to meet the real George Kaplan. She instructs him to take a bus to a deserted prairie stop.

8a. Protagonist's First Growth (45)

At the prairie stop, Thornhill waits for Kaplan. A crop-duster-plane appears and machine guns open fire. Stripped of all his protection and assets, Thornhill is chased by the crop-duster and has to run for his life. He escapes when the plane crashes into a gasoline truck.

9. Midpoint/Point of No Return (60)

Going to the Ambassador Hotel in Chicago in search of Eve, Thornhill realizes that she set him up and tried to send him to his death.

10. Bad Guys Close In (61-75):

Thornhill follows Eve to an auction house where Vandamm is bidding for a pre-Colombian statue. Vandamm's heavies close in on Thornhill at the auction house and he escapes by bidding crazily in order to get himself arrested. After the police arrest him for being a public nuisance, the Professor bails him out.

11. All Is Lost (75):

The Professor tells Thornhill that Eve is really working for the government and that Thornhill's resistance to playing the role of George Kaplan has unwittingly put Eve's life in danger. Eve shoots Thornhill with fake bullets to persuade Vandamm to take her away with him. Thornhill's "body" is taken to the local hospital to convince Vandamm that Kaplan is dead.

12. Dark Night of the Soul (75-85):

Thornhill finds out from the Professor that Eve is planning to go away with Vandamm to extract government information from him. One of the Professor's men knocks Thornhill out and Eve goes ahead with the plan.

13. Act Two Turning Point/Break into Three (85-90):

Thornhill escapes from the hospital where he is being held to go and rescue Eve.

13a. (91-105) Wrap-up loose strings and subplots

One of Vandamm's henchmen, Leonard (Martin Landau), finds out that Eve is really a double agent when he discovers the blank bullets and tells Vandamm. Vandamm decides to dispose of Eve. Thornhill breaks into Vandamm's house near Mount Rushmore to try and warn Eve that Vandamm is on to her.

14. Final Showdown/Climax (105-118):

Thornill rescues Eve, who grabs the pre-Colombian statue from Vandamm and she and Thornill are chased across Mount Rushmore.

14a. Tag/Denouement — Fast Wrap-up subplots (119-120)

Eve slips off a ledge on Mount Rushmore and Thornhill holds onto her for dear life. Leonard tries to kill them both, but is shot by the police and falls to his death.

15. Final Image (120):

A changed Thornhill, now ready to commit, pulls Eve on board the 20th Century Limited, saying "Come along, Mrs. Thornhill" and the final shot is a phallic joke — a shot of the train entering a tunnel.

BREAKING IT DOWN INTO SCENES

Once you have the beats for your movie, you then need to break it down into individual scenes. John Michael Hayes wrote the first treatment of *Rear Window* on his own. After making corrections, he cut the draft down as he had a tendency to write long. Then he sat down with Hitchcock with the second draft and had 200–300 numbered shots. By the time they had finished, that number had increased to 600 shots, as Hitch would break it up and sketch the camera angles from his director's viewpoint. He thought intensely about a scene and inserted suspense where audiences least expected it.

Hitchcock said his own primary contribution to a film occurred while the script was being written. Before going into the studio to film, Hitchcock liked to have the whole film completely in his mind, shot by shot on paper, and that meant working a lot on the script before he even entered the studio. "Once the screenplay is finished," he said, "I'd just as soon not make the film at all. All the fun is over. I have a strongly visual mind. I visualize a picture right down to the final cuts. I write all this out in the greatest detail in the script, and then I don't look at the script while I'm shooting. I know it off by heart, just as an orchestra conductor needs not look at the score."

He would often say that if it was in the script he would shoot it, but if it wasn't he wouldn't. Hitchcock believed that the most important part of the shooting was done on paper and tended to advertise that he found actual shooting to be tedious, although at least some of this attitude was simply Hitch's droll sense of humor.

KNOW YOUR AUDIENCE

" I enjoy playing the audience like a piano. "
— Alfred Hitchcock

When writing your script, you have to ask yourself: What is the audience thinking now? And you'd better make sure they are thinking the way you want them to think, not the way they want to think. For Hitchcock, knowing your audience when writing your screenplay was all-important. Make sure that the content engages them and reels them in. Use characters to tease the viewer and pull them along, desperately wanting more. "I think a director should understand the psychology of audiences," said Hitchcock. Know the psychology of your audience — especially what they fear.

Hitchcock knew why people are drawn to a darkened movie theater to absorb themselves for hours with images on a screen. They do it to have fun, in the same way that people go on a roller coaster ride to be thrilled. "Look at the people who pay money to go on the roller coaster, or to see the haunted house," Hitchcock said, "to make themselves scream is a form of pleasure that people will pay for." As a film director he knew that he could throw birds at his audience, force them to witness murder, or pull them into an obsessive love story, and that they knew nothing harmful would actually happen to them. They're confident that they'll be able to walk out the exit when it's done and resume their normal lives. As Hitchcock said with a wink, "Always make the audience suffer as much as possible." The more fun they have "suffering," the quicker they will come back for more. There will be more about knowing your audience in Chapter 8 on marketing.

TRUST YOUR SPOUSE

> *" The first of the four is a film editor, the second is a script writer, the third is the mother of my daughter Pat, and the fourth is a finer cook that has ever performed miracles in a domestic kitchen — and [all four of] their names are Alma Reville. " — Alfred Hitchcock on his most important collaborators*

A very important confidante and collaborator was Hitchcock's wife, Alma. They met while she was working as an editor in England in 1921, and over a 54-year-old marriage enjoyed a fruitful collaboration where she would advise on scripts and editing. Under her maiden name Alma Reville she earned a story credit on sixteen of Hitchcock's films, but collaborated on far more. When they first met, Alma was working as a film editor on a silent movie called *Woman to Woman* (1923). Hitchcock had been hired to design the title cards, but he never spoke to her, as he later confessed, out of shyness. Two years later, after he had been promoted to director and she to assistant director, he asked Alma to be his editor. They married in 1926, and she was a constant in Hitchcock's life and career. Hitchcock often deferred decisions on script changes, saying, "I'll discuss it with Madame."

WRITING DIALOGUE

> *" Dialogue is something that comes out of the mouths of people who are telling a visual story. " — Alfred Hitchcock*

The best Hitchcock films crackle with sparkling dialogue and witty repartee. Cary Grant and Ingrid Bergman put duty before love in *Notorious*. Thelma Ritter wisecracks to James Stewart in *Rear Window*. Cary Grant's dialogue in *North by Northwest* is that of a fast-talking, slick Madison Avenue advertising exec. After setting out the scenes, dialogue is the next phase in the scriptwriting process. Once the storyline is decided upon and the screenwriter takes over, Hitchcock dealt with it sequence by sequence. You start the first sequence in the treatment, and build it up as you go along.

Hitchcock began in silent films, and had a tendency to rely on the camera to tell his story visually as much as he could. He believed that dialogue should be part of the atmosphere and not the focal point. He'd pass his knowledge to his writers, so that they too knew how to tell a story visually rather than relying on words. Writing dialogue is a job on its own, and it comes out of character. Hitch knew that and couldn't be a jack-of-all-trades as he was busy putting the images on screen, so he left the task of writing dialogue to his screenwriters.

Two of his best writers, John Michael Hayes and Ernest Lehman, specialized in writing dialogue. John Michael Hayes' career started as a radio writer, and he wrote the screenplay for four Hitchcock films. When he met Hitchcock for the first time, they didn't talk about *Rear Window*, the movie they were about to make. Later, Hitch told Hayes why he hired him: "You talked a lot, and on the assumption that a man who talks a lot has something to say, I hired you." Hayes' scripts are prized for their unique blend of sophisticated repartee and colloquial banter, and he said that Hitchcock let him write on his own and then would confer afterwards.

WRITING SUBTEXT

" Puns are the highest forms of literature. "
— *Alfred Hitchcock*

Good writing is subtext, reading between the lines, rather than "on the nose" dialogue. Much of the dialogue in Hitchcock's best screenplays, such as *Notorious, Rear Window*, and *North by Northwest*, is indirect, with layers of meaning. Nobody says anything straight; the dialogue is oblique, but perfectly understandable. It's more challenging to write subtext, and it's more interesting to say things through a literary device and have people remember the lines. Often Hitchcock writers John Michael Hayes and Ernest Lehman had their best and most memorable lines quoted back to them by the public.

Ernest Lehman's screenplay for *North by Northwest* sparkles with witty dialogue, with more funny lines than most comedies. He describes his dialogue as "repartee" and there are pages and pages of it in the film. This is why he chose Cary Grant's character to be a fast-talking advertising man, so that he could talk in a kind of clever banter, rather than speaking in a straightforward manner. Lehman felt that this would be more amusing and that it was dialogue that Cary Grant could do very well, which is why he was cast over another Hitchcock regular, James Stewart. Stewart, with his slow homespun drawl, would have taken four hours to say all the lines in the picture!

One of Lehman's favorite lines in the *North by Northwest* script is when Thornhill says to Eve, "How does a girl like you get to be a girl like you?" Another memorable line occurs at the end of the movie, when the rangers shoot Vandamm's henchman Leonard, and Vandamm says dryly, "That's not very sporting, using real bullets."

Good dialogue must be full of conflict, and have a rhythm that's easily spoken. Just like Guy Haines' (Farley Granger) epic tennis match in *Strangers on a Train*, verbal

Alfred Hitchcock with his leading man, Cary Grant, on location for *North by Northwest* (1959).

exchanges should move back and forth between characters, shifting power from one side to the other, until somebody scores the point. The focus of the scene should never be on what the characters are actually saying. Have something else going on. Resort to dialogue only when it's impossible to do otherwise.

One of your characters could be pre-occupied with something during a dialogue scene. Their eyes can then be distracted while the other person doesn't notice. This is a good way to pull the audience into a character's secretive world. As Hitchcock observed, "People don't often always express their inner thoughts to one another; a conversation might be quite trivial, but often the eyes reveal what a person thinks or feels." Just like in real life.

Hitchcock loved counterpoint dialogue and contrast. In *Notorious*, Alicia and Devlin (Ingrid Bergman and Cary Grant) talk about a chicken dinner and who is going to wash the dishes afterwards, all while continuously kissing. One of the best-written scenes in *The Birds* is where the townspeople take shelter in a restaurant and offer divergent opinions about why the birds are attacking. The scene is echoed in M. Night Shyamalan's *The Happening* (2008) when everyone is holed up in the diner, and also in Frank Darabont's *The Mist* (2007) when the townspeople take refuge in a supermarket.

WRITER'S BLOCK

" When we tell a story in cinema, we should resort to dialogue only when it's impossible to do otherwise. " — Alfred Hitchcock

It happens to the best of us. You're in front of your computer staring at a blank screen, not knowing how to write a particular scene. You know how it starts and you know where it needs to go, but you have no idea how to get there. You'll sit at your desk for hours, but have nothing to show for it at the end of the day. Yes, it's the dreaded writer's block.

Take comfort that Hitchcock and his best writers also suffered from writer's block at times. As Ernest Lehman said, "Movie writing is all about one thing...despair." Along with despair, writing is all about solving problems. On *North by Northwest*, Lehman was always trying to write himself out of corners. "You try every possible option until the right one hits," he said.

When Lehman turned in 65 pages of screenplay for the first act of *North by Northwest*, Hitchcock loved it and pitched it the MGM execs as is. Everything in the story was moving in a northwesterly direction towards Hitchcock's original idea of Cary Grant running across the faces on Mount Rushmore. But when it came to actually writing the last act, Lehman didn't know how to resolve the film. He called Hitchcock over to his office, and the two sat looking at each other glumly. Then for some reason Lehman said, "She takes a gun out of her purse and shoots him."

Hitchcock seized upon this and replied, "I can see Cary falling over and landing on the table." Lehman added, "They are fake bullets!" And from that they built the entire third act for *North by Northwest*. Eve shoots Thornhill and then the Professor hides him, so the heavies think he has been killed, which solidifies Eve's position with bad guy Vandamm, and then Thornhill goes to rescue Eve. Hitchcock elaborated that the Polish Resistance used to shoot members of their own people to prove that they were not members. In the same way, Eve "shoots" Thornhill with fake bullets so that Vandamm will take her away with him and not be suspicious that she really is a double agent.

WRITE FOR COMEDY

" There wasn't a single critic who had a sense of humor about Psycho, *which makes them very dull people to me. " — Alfred Hitchcock*

Hitchcock, as well as looking for stories with plenty of action, had a dark, macabre sense of humor and relished tales where he could inject his sense of fun. Through his quirky characters, ironic situations, and a complex balance of laughs and tension, Hitchcock found a way to make his suspense unbearably fun for his audiences. He famously called *Psycho* a "fun picture," and in *The Trouble With Harry* (1955) he turned the subject of an inconvenient dead body into lightweight comedy.

A successful movie juxtaposes tension and relaxation, and relieves horror with humor. After a certain amount of suspense, Hitchcock believed that an audience must find relief in laughter, so he used comedy to supply a definite contrast. He takes a dramatic situation up and up to its peak of excitement and then, before it has time to start the downward curve, he introduces comedy to relieve the tension. Then he feels safe with the climax. If the movie comes to an end without any contrast, the climax would probably turn into an anti-climax.

The fact that Hitchcock called *Psycho* a fun picture just goes to show how sophisticated he was. "The content of such I found rather amusing and I thought it was big joke, you know. And I was horrified to find that some people took it seriously. It was intended for people to scream and yell," said Hitch. It's Hitchcock's humor that makes him able to tackle the outrageousness of it — if he told the same story seriously, then it would be a case history rather than a suspense film. He thought that you must have a sense of humor if you are scaring people, and although *Psycho* has no obvious laughs, Hitchcock intended it to be funny. There are some very funny lines in the picture, such as when Norman apologizes for his mother's screaming outburst, overheard by Marion, with "Mother — um — What is the phrase? — She isn't quite herself today." ("Mother," of course, is really Norman.)

One of the best examples of Hitchcock's whimsical use of setting to create comedy is in *The Trouble With Harry.* All is normal in this small town with green meadows, sunshine, and orange autumn leaves, until a dead body shows up. The question then raised is what can be done with a dead body? Hitchcock always said that the film was very personal to him, because it involved his own sense of the macabre. One of his favorite lines in the movie comes when Captain Wiles (Edmund Gwenn) is dragging the dead body by the legs like a wheelbarrow, and a spinster comes up and says matter-of-factly, "What seems to be the trouble, Captain?"

Hitchcock's anecdote from *The Trouble With Harry* shows that in any real-life situation, no matter how serious, if you look hard enough, you're sure to find the comedy. He used comedy for light relief and contrast, especially in dark or serious subjects. When he made *The 39 Steps*, he was determined to show every angle of each situation. "It may have been tragic or it may have been dramatic, but, looked at in another way, it was comic." So Hitchcock put many comic touches in the film, such as the complications arising when an unmarried couple, handcuffed together, must spend a night together in a shared bed.

Other films such as *Saboteur* (1942), *Shadow of a Doubt* (1943), and *Strangers on a Train* (1951) are sprinkled with macabre humor. *Rear Window* (1954) is a film where not much action happens, as the wheelchair-bound main character is confined to his apartment with a broken leg and serious suspicions about a possibly murderous neighbor. But it has some great moments of comedy, partly due

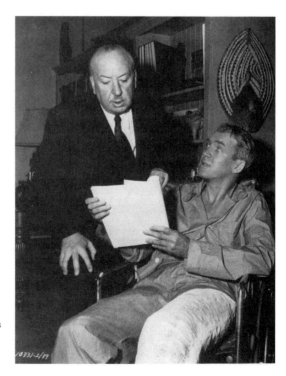

Alfred Hitchcock and James Stewart discuss a scene on the set of ***Rear Window*** **(1954).**

to the cracking dialogue delivered between the man and his sarcastic nurse.

At the same time, comedy needs to be used in the right places and in the right ways so that it doesn't undermine the suspense. The audience must take the suspense seriously, be emotionally involved, and the wrong kind of comedy that takes us out of our emotional connection at the wrong moment will kill suspense. As director John Schlesinger said of Hitchcock, "I can think of no other director who has combined suspense, irony, and humor into such extraordinary results."

USE COUNTERPOINT AND CONTRAST

"In the mystery and suspense genre, a tongue-in-cheek approach is indispensable."
— *Alfred Hitchcock*

Humor is essential to Hitchcock when storytelling and was often used as counterpoint during times of dramatic situations. Comedy and laughter doesn't diminish how effective and suspenseful a situation is but heightens the drama and makes it more potent. "For me, suspense doesn't have any value unless it's balanced by humor," said Hitchcock. So comedy can make your film more dramatic, because it offers contrast and gives the audience a chance to reflect. If the film is dramatic or tragic, the obvious contrast is comedy.

Often Hitchcock had two things happening at once. He built tension into a scene by using contrasting situations, with two unrelated things happening simultaneously. The audience should be focused on the momentum of one, and be interrupted by the other. Usually the second item should be a humorous distraction that means nothing, and this can often be dialogue.

In *Spellbound* (1945), Dr. Constance Petersen (Ingrid Bergman) sees a note that has been slipped under her door. Just when she goes to reach for it, the door opens and nosy colleagues step in to speak with her about the disappearance of her patient, completely unaware that they are standing on top of a note from him. The audience anxiously waits to see if they notice the note before Constance can get to it. The end result: the simple act of a character reaching for a note has been turned into a nail-biter through contrast.

When unexpected guests arrive at the London hotel room in *The Man Who Knew Too Much*, Ben and Jo (Jimmy Stewart and Doris Day) are in the midst of a tense phone call as they search for their kidnapped son. The arrival of the guests, old friends who are laughing and joking, serves as dramatic counterpoint to the real momentum of the scene.

Hitchcock also used comedy to contrast his characters with their situation. He often took glamorous and sophisticated characters like Connie Porter (Tallulah Bankhead) in *Lifeboat*, Roger Thornhill (Cary Grant) in *North by Northwest*, and Melanie Daniels (Tippi Hedren) in *The Birds*, and made them more comic through the contrast of often brutal situations. In doing so, he kept the whole film on a human level, with emotions mixed in the incongruous way they are in real life. He let the characters tell the story, and some of the most interesting scenes between the characters are the dialogue scenes that arise. Conversations between Hitchcock characters can be long, but they are never dull.

In *Frenzy*, Hitchcock liked the extremes between comedy and horror, especially the broad humor in the dinner scenes. He used humor to great effect between the chief inspector, played by Alec McCowen, and his wife, played by Vivien Merchant. "I invented the chief inspector's wife so as to permit myself to place most of the discussion of the crime outside a professional context," said Hitchcock. "And I get comedy to sugar-coat the discussions by making the wife a gourmet cook. So this inspector comes home every night to discussion of the murders over rich meals."

Alec McCowen remembers filming the scene in just two days, and that Hitchcock gave very little direction to himself and Vivien Merchant, allowing them to improvise the comedy. Many of the dialogues scenes only needed one take, and with the comedy Hitchcock encouraged screenwriter Anthony Schaffer to play it up. Hitchcock himself was very pleased with the results, as he described it as, "Two beautiful performers doing it with such understatement, a favorite with me is to get the maximum result with the minimum of effort." The humor in *Frenzy* was true in its setting and character.

This contrasts with the severity and gruesomeness of the rest of *Frenzy*, especially when Barry Foster, playing the necktie murderer, disposes of his latest victim by carrying her body in a potato sack and dumping it onto the back of a truck. He then realizes that his necktie pin is clasped in her dead fingers and has to go back and retrieve it. It's "funny and horrible," as Hitchcock described it, at the same time. You have the sweat of the murderer as he tries to retrieve his necktie pin from the fingers of his dead victim, which he has to snap like breadsticks. As director Guillermo del Toro says, "The scene is pregnant with morbid sensuality and vitriolic humor. It remains one of the most sincere hints into the darkest side of Hitchcock."

EXPOSITION AND DIALOGUE

"Exposition is a pill that must be sugar-coated." — Alfred Hitchcock

One of the cardinal sins for a writer to say in order to get themselves out of trouble is, "We will cover that with a line of dialogue." Exposition. It's something that most writers and filmmakers dread. Countless scriptwriting classes have taught us that exposition is dull, unnecessary, un-cinematic, time wasting, and that you should try to avoid devoting large numbers of screen pages to character exposition. Where exposition is necessary, where you are telling the audience important information, you should at all times try other means to convey it first. "By the time you give it, it must appear to be something else," said Hitchcock.

" Drama is life with the dull bits cut out. "
— *Alfred Hitchcock*

Everything in your story should be streamlined. If your story is confusing or requires a lot memory, you're never going to get suspense out of it. The key to creating the Hitchcock touch is to keep your stories simple and linear so that the audience can easily follow along. Get rid of those extraneous scenes that don't move the story forward. Hitchcock called these scenes "non-scenes," which have no dramatic purpose. Each scene should include only those essential ingredients that make things gripping for the audience.

In *North by Northwest*, Hitchcock uses exposition after Roger Thornhill is mistaken for the non-existent agent George Kaplan and is on the run from the police. The Professor explains to his colleagues (and us) that Thornhill has been mistaken for a decoy spy who actually doesn't exist. Hitchcock inserted this scene so that the audience could enjoy the rest of the story and go along with the ride. Although this explanation scene was necessary, Hitchcock was sure that it should not come at the opening of the movie, but come at a point "when you were accounting for a number of strange and bizarre events."

" A critic who talks to me about plausibility is a dull fellow. " — *Alfred Hitchcock*

Often Hitchcock was criticized for his films lacking plausibility and stretching credibility. But he thought that plausibility for the sake of plausibility doesn't help. It's a waste of time. If you want to analyze everything in terms of plausibility, then you end up doing a documentary. In a documentary, real life has created the basic material for you, but in a fiction movie, you must create life, and from that comes matters of impression, expression, and point of view, and so long as it's not dull, you have free reign to do whatever you like — plausibly or not.

HAVE A SURPRISE ENDING

Everyone loves a surprise ending. There's nothing more satisfying than walking out of the movie theatre saying to yourself, "I wish I had seen that coming sooner." It gives the film a lasting appeal and leaves you feeling satisfied. Once you've built your audience into gripping suspense, never end the movie the way they expect. Lead them in one direction and then pull the rug out from under them in a surprise twist.

In the climactic scene of *Saboteur*, the villain is cornered on the top of the Statue of Liberty as the hero holds him at gunpoint. When the hero begins to speak, he startles the villain, who falls backwards over the edge. A similar thing happens at the end of *Vertigo*. Scottie has dragged Judy up to the top of the bell tower after discovering that she and his lost love Madeleine are the same girl. Just as it looks like the two will finally be reconciled, the sudden appearance of a nun sends Judy falling over the edge and to her death. At the end of *Psycho*, when Lila explores the Bates house, she discovers the horrifying secrets behind Mrs. Bates. As Tom Holland, who directed *Fright Night* (1985) and *Child's Play* (1988) says, "Miss Crane turns the chair in the basement in *Psycho* to see the mother who she and all of us thought was alive is nothing more than a stuffed, desiccated corpse. Great reveal."

Some recent Hitchcockian thrillers with a final twist include *The Crying Game* (1992), *The Usual Suspects* (1995), *Se7en* (1995), *The Sixth Sense* (1999), *Memento* (2000), and *The Others* (2001).

The twist keeps the audience glued to their seats in anticipation. Your story should also be upfront about the content, but have a few twists and turns to keep the reader or viewer wanting to know more.

THE "ICE BOX SYNDROME"

You don't always have to wrap everything up in a neat bundle at the end of your movie. Sometimes it's better to leave things unresolved. Hitchcock called this the "Ice Box Syndrome," referring to the moment when a couple returns home from the movies and they discuss the plot, and something is troubling them, they'll reach into their "ice box" (refrigerator). "I leave holes in my films deliberately, so that the following scenario can take place in countless homes," said Hitchcock. "The man of the house gets out of bed in the middle of the night, and goes downstairs and takes a chicken leg out of the ice box. His wife follows him down and asks what he's doing. 'You know,' he says, 'there's a hole in that film we saw tonight.' 'No there isn't,' she says and they fall to arguing. As a result of which they go to see it again."

Vertigo is full of Ice Box Syndromes, which may be part of its enduring appeal to mystery lovers. We never discover how Scottie — whom we first meet as he's dangling precariously from a roof — managed to escape from falling to his death, or if Gavin Elster, the murderer, is caught, or how Judy/Madeleine managed to leave the hotel without Scottie finding out. Similarly in *The Birds*, the audience never learns why the birds are attacking or if the main characters successfully escape.

When writing *Frenzy*, screenwriter Anthony Schaffer asked Hitchcock "How many Ice Box Syndromes do you want me to put into the screenplay?" Some of Hitchcock's best films were full of refrigerator talk.

CLOSE YOUR EYES AND VISUALIZE

" I think one of the biggest problems that we have in our business is the inability of people to visualize. "— Alfred Hitchcock

Hitchcock famously never looked through the camera, because he could visualize what he saw. It's not what the camera sees, it's what you see on the screen, the succession of images. For Hitchcock, the visual is the most vital element in the cinema, especially when writing a screenplay. It's more than writing about words. Hitchcock always tried to tell the story in cinematic terms, not in endless talk. He was a purist and believed that film is a succession of images on the screen; this in turn creates ideas, which in turn creates emotion, which only seldom leads to dialogue.

He also believed that not enough visualizing was done in studios, and instead far too much writing. A movie writer types a lot of dialogue in his word processor and becomes satisfied with that day's work. There is also a growing habit of reading a film script by the dialogue alone. Hitchcock deplored this method, which he saw as lazy neglect.

Effective visualizing occurs during the opening of *Rear Window*, an example of Hitchcock working beautifully with his writer John Michael Hayes. Hitchcock uses a succession of images of items around L.B. Jeffries' apartment to tell the story of how he came to break his leg, why he's in a wheelchair, and what his occupation is. All this is done with the use of the visual rather than dialogue. In Hitch's 1956 version of *The Man Who Knew Too Much*, in the scene at the Albert Hall with James Stewart and Doris Day, Hitchcock and his writer Hayes had written dialogue for Stewart to say when he chases Day up the stairs in the climactic sequence. But Hitchcock felt that without dialogue, this whole final sequence where the assassination is about to take place — of a central figure from some nameless country — would be stronger. He discovered that he didn't need the dialogue at all.

EXERCISES

1. Take your idea for a movie from Chapter 1 and break it down into outline and treatment. Try and concentrate on the visuals and have no dialogue at all. This will help you practice telling a story through images.

2. Close your eyes and visualize the scenes in your treatment. What images come to mind and how do you plan to film them?

3. Write down some memorable dialogue exchanges from three Hitchcock films: *Rear Window*, *To Catch a Thief*, and *North by Northwest*. What does the dialogue say about the characters who are speaking?

4. Watch *The 39 Steps* and *North by Northwest*. How do the screenplays compare and what similarities can you see? Can you recognize the beats which are identical in each movie?

5. Write out the scenes of your screenplay on cards. Try putting each beat or scene on a card to help you anchor down your plot points before you write up the scene-by-scene outline. If one scene isn't working where it is, try shuffling your cards around until you find a structure that works.

6. Think about subtext in a Hitchcock movie. What are the characters saying and what are they really saying during the balcony scene between Alicia and Devlin in *Notorious*, the parlor scene between Marion and

Norman in *Psycho*, the dinner in the women's club between Richard Blaney and Brenda in *Frenzy*? How does the subtext add to the theme of the movie?

7. Take some recent films that have a big twist at the end. How does the director prepare any visual or verbal clues to the twist?

8. Pretend that you are playing a practical joke on the main character of your movie. Give him the most ironic situations to deal with — the unexpected gag, the coincidence, the worst possible thing that can go wrong. Show how this contrast can be used to build tension.

Key Hitchcock films to watch

The 39 Steps (1935)
Notorious (1946)
Rear Window (1954)
To Catch a Thief (1955)
The Man Who Knew Too Much (1956)
North by Northwest (1959)
Psycho (1960)

Other directors' films to watch

The Crying Game (1992)
Four Weddings and a Funeral (1994)
Pulp Fiction (1994)
The Usual Suspects (1995)
The Sixth Sense (1999)

Further reading

Making a Good Script Great (1994) by Linda Seger
Hitchcock on Hitchcock (1997) by Sidney Gottleib
Save the Cat! (2005) by Blake Snyder

CHAPTER THREE

PRE-PRODUCTION

> **"** *I have been an art director, I've written scripts, I've been an assistant director, a production manager, I've even turned a camera, lit, I've done every job that is to be done on the set.* **"** — *Alfred Hitchcock*

Hitchcock was famous for pre-planning all his movies, even to the extent of storyboarding every shot. Pre-production is an important part of movie-making, as it gives the director the opportunity to sit down with the art designer, the storyboard artist, the costume designer, and the assistant director, etc., to plan in detail the design of the film. The French word for this stage is *mise-en-scène*. For Hitchcock this means all the visual elements including what is seen on the set and how the camera portrays the scene. He himself began his film career in the art department, as a writer and designer of movie titles, and he never forgot the power of design to attract an audience. When he worked as an art director, Hitchcock was dogmatic, "I would build the set and say here's where it's shot from. I would tell the director." Hitchcock devoted himself to learning his trade, and within five short years, encouraged by studio head Michael Balcon of Famous Players-Lasky, he had worked his way around the studio's many departments. Within a couple of years of learning, he began working as an assistant director.

WORK WITH A PRODUCTION DESIGNER

When writing a script, Hitchcock invited the production designer very early on to sit with him and the writer. The production designer is responsible for the space in which the movie takes place and will take a sequence and through a series of sketches indicate camera set-ups, design angles, and production ideas. Hitchcock worked with some of the best designers in the business, including Robert Boyle on *Saboteur*, *North by Northwest*, *The Birds*, and *Marnie*, and Henry Bumstead on *Vertigo* and *Family Plot*. These designers created the extraordinary sets for some of Hitchcock's greatest films, including dizzying staircases, opulent hotels, a recreation of the top of the Statue of Liberty, Mount Rushmore, and exotic locations like Morocco and the South of France.

In designing a scene, Hitchcock would say, "What sort of setting should we write this for?" During the course of writing he wanted certain things researched to see if they were possible. If they don't work out, he didn't put them in the script. So the designer is very much involved in the making of the film as well. Hitchcock always took great care to be accurate in detail no matter how fantastic the situation might be. In the making of *The Birds*, despite the extraordinary premise of birds attacking humans, Hitchcock sought documentary realism by having every man, woman and child in Bodega Bay photographed to see what they wore. He also researched the houses of the characters, making sure, for example, that he got authentic details for the schoolteacher. That's why his films have often been described as dreams; while they have an element of fantasy, they also appear to be so realistic.

CHANGE YOUR LOCATIONS OFTEN

Hitchcock's films feature a wide variety of glamorous locations. There are the picture postcard settings of the South of France in *To Catch a Thief*, exotic Marrakech in the remake of *The Man Who Knew Too Much*, the hilly streets of San Francisco in *Vertigo*, and Moscow, New York, Paris, and Cuba in *Topaz*. Many of his films were shown in glorious Technicolor and VistaVision, transporting the viewer to exotic and faraway locations, at a time when movie theatre managers were keen to woo audiences from television. Hitchcock knew that one of the ways in which the suspense drama must change is in its setting. The Orient Express, for example, has had its day as a scene for spy melodrama. The same could be true for narrow stairways, high towers, and dark subways. So Hitchcock had to be inventive in his backgrounds and settings and changed his locations often in his movies.

In *North by Northwest*, Roger Thornhill's adventures start in Manhattan at the Plaza Hotel, a mansion on Long Island, the United Nations building, and Grand Central Station. Then he proceeds to Chicago, a prairie stop in Indiana, and finally Mount Rushmore National Park. *North by Northwest* was Hitchcock's way of covering America in the same way he had done with England and Scotland in *The 39 Steps*. He had always wanted to film on Mount Rushmore and *North by Northwest* is a summary of all his American work. As Hitchcock was an art student before he took up directing films, he even thought about the backgrounds of his stories first. That's how his first version of *The Man Who Knew Too Much* (1934) started. Hitchcock looked at the snowy Alps and the dingy London alleys, and into those backgrounds he threw characters into the middle for contrast.

Today's action thrillers have taken a tip from Hitchcock, such as the *Bourne* and *Mission: Impossible* films, where there are many glamorous locales that change often. In *The Bourne Ultimatum* (2007), the action switches from Madrid to Tangier to New York, and in *Mission: Impossible – Ghost Protocol* (2011), Tom Cruise leads his team from Moscow to Dubai to India. By changing your movie locations frequently, with plenty of action, the audience won't have the chance to get bored.

MAKE YOUR LOCATIONS WORK DRAMATICALLY

"When I go for a locale, it must be used dramatically." — *Alfred Hitchcock*

When choosing your locations for your movie, think how they can be used dramatically. Hitchcock believed that if you are using a unique location, it should be used to its utmost. He was adamant that the backgrounds must be incorporated into the drama and made it a rule to exploit elements that are connected with a location, otherwise he felt like he'd missed out on making maximum use of the setting. Never use a setting simply as a background. Use it 100%.

The first version of *The Man Who Knew Too Much* was filmed in Switzerland and the opening was based on Hitch's frequent trips to St. Moritz. He thought about what there was in Switzerland and decided that everything in the film should be relevant to the country. So the location went from being beyond a mere background to being used dramatically as well. A chocolate factory turned out to be a nest for spies, the lakes were used for drowning, the Alps for people falling off, and the chocolate for choking on.

In *Foreign Correspondent* (1940) the use of the windmills is a good example of using your locations dramatically. Just like in Switzerland, it's essential to say, well I'm in Holland, what have they got in Holland? Tulips? Windmills? The windmills in the movie aren't just scenery, they become part of the plot — a windmill is turning the wrong way as a signal as to where a person is being held captive.

Roger Thornhill is trapped in an auction room in *North by Northwest* and can't get out. Bad guys are closing in on him and if they catch him they will kill him. Hitchcock and his writer Ernest Lehman thought about the question "How could he get out?" The only way for Thornhill to escape would be through crazy bidding, which would create a public disturbance. The essential point is that Hitchcock used the background of an auction

Heavies are closing in at an auction, so Roger Thornhill (Cary Grant) deliberately gets himself arrested in order to escape. (*North by Northwest*, 1959)

room as part of the story and the suspense. It isn't just a background.

Towards the end of *Torn Curtain* (1966), Michael Armstrong (Paul Newman) goes to a ballet along with his fiancée Sarah (Julie Andrews). Who discovers him but a ballerina, in the middle of her dance, during a pirouette. How does he get the idea to shout "Fire!" to escape the bad guys? From a scenic fire on the stage. So Hitchcock integrates the ballet into the plot and makes the setting work dramatically.

USE YOUR PROPS DRAMATICALLY

"It's merely a matter of utilizing your materials to the fullest dramatic extent." — *Alfred Hitchcock*

It's not just the location that Hitchcock used to the fullest dramatic extent, but the props inside the location as well. About a third of the way into *Torn Curtain*, Michael goes to an isolated farmhouse to meet his contact from Pi, a secret underground resistance movement. Here Hitchcock makes memorable use of the setting, as all the tools in the farmhouse became tools of death or torture, such as a knife, a shovel, and a gas oven. "Some of our most exquisite murders have been domestic, performed with tenderness in simple, homey places like the kitchen table," said Hitchcock.

In *Rear Window*, when Lars Thorwald (Raymond Burr), the neighbor L.B. Jeffries (James Stewart) has been spying on, comes into Jeffries' apartment, Jeffries temporarily fends Thorwald off using the strong flashbulbs in his camera. Jeffries is a photographer, so Hitchcock insists on using those elements that belong to the character. Hitchcock said, "I always do, as far as I can, use part of the background in the action of the story." Otherwise he felt that he's neglecting something if he's not using them.

Frenzy takes place against a backdrop of Covent Garden, a famous produce market in London, where the necktie murderer Rusk (Barry Foster) is a fruit and vegetable merchant. When Rusk hides his latest victim in a potato truck, Hitchcock uses the milieu to the fullest and it evens provides the clues to solving the murder. The body is later found covered with potato dust, and a clothes brush Rusk uses implicates him in the crime. "Thanks to the potato dust one says to oneself that perhaps the police will discover a trail that will lead them to the true criminal," said Hitch. If *Frenzy* had not been made in Covent Garden, the man may not have been arrested, because it ended up in potato dust. So the market really functioned as a character in the film.

AVOID THE CLICHÉ IN YOUR LOCATIONS

" That's what life is all about today, avoiding the cliché. " — Alfred Hitchcock

Another pitfall to avoid is the cliché. Hitchcock spent half of his time avoiding the cliché when writing scenes, so that his movies were fresh and inventive. While writing *North by Northwest*, Ernest Lehman would come up with an idea and Hitch would often say, "Oh, that's the way they do it in the movies!"

There's the familiar scene of a man being told to go to a spot and there the audience suspects he will be shot. In most films the setting will be night, and a corner of the street, where the man stands under the streetlights. A black cat may run along the wall, creating an atmosphere of terror. The audience waits for the black limousine to arrive. That's the cliché. Indeed that's a scene straight out of Carol Reed's *The Third Man* (1949).

Hitchcock wanted the opposite of that cliché for the scene in *North by Northwest* where Roger Thornill is

There's no hiding in broad daylight for Roger Thornhill (Cary Grant) as he's chased by a crop-duster in *North by Northwest* (1959).

chased by the crop-duster. It's essentially the same scene as the man waiting under the streetlight, but this time there is no darkness, and everything is in bright sunlight. We don't see anything, no houses, nothing. Thornhill stands alone and waits. Then Hitchcock brings on the cliché, the menacing black car, but it goes away. The audience says it can't be the car, what is it? Now comes an old car. A man gets out, but the man says "That's funny. That plane's dusting crops in a place where there ain't no crops." And with that Thornhill, and the audience, finally realizes where the threat will be coming from.

It's important in stories such as these, with sinister implications, to use counterpoint, and to have great contrasts between situation and background. Just like Hitchcock avoided the cliché in the crop-duster sequence of *North by Northwest*. He believed that for his dramas to be strong, they must be set in non-clichéd environments of high contrast.

In *Rope* he chose a light, beautifully appointed apartment as the setting for a terrible murder. The audience witnesses two university students (played by John Dall and Farley Granger) strangle a friend to prove an intellectual exercise, and then hide the body inside a chest on which they then serve a dinner party. Throughout one student is charming and gracious as the host, and his apartment is tastefully decorated (supplemented with some of Hitchcock's own artwork). "How cozy" remarks one of the guests. Later, when the other student plays the piano, he picks a light and childish piece — a minuet. For Hitchcock, the best suspense involves contrast.

In contrast to the dark, urban *noir* films of its time, evil is found in broad daylight, lurking beneath the surface of a small American town in *Shadow of a Doubt* (1943), a film that turned the whole suspense genre on its head. It was one of the most satisfying films for Hitchcock because character and location combined to enhance the plot. "For once there was time to get characters into it," said Hitchcock, which is one of the reasons why he describes *Shadow of a Doubt* as his favorite of his films. Thornton Wilder wrote the screenplay in Hollywood, but before a line was written, he and Hitch spent some time in Northern California, going to the film's setting of Santa Rosa so that they were familiar with the feel of the whole town and its people.

Hitchcock and Wilder captured the ordinary life of small-town America and it was Wilder who came up with the idea of the "Merry Widower Murderer," introducing the element of evil into this idyllic setting. Santa Rosa itself becomes a character in the film; from the house the Newton family lives in to the busy intersection with the traffic cop, from the local bank to the public library. It's a typical All-American provincial town with gossip and secrets, and Uncle Charlie and Emma Newton are nostalgic for their own childhood and the street where they grew up.

Hitchcock would portray small-town life again to the same effect years later in *The Birds* (1963). Both films have a sense of character and place that are a contrast to the frightening goings-on of their plots. This suburban setting has laid the groundwork for other spooky suburban locales in movies such as *Halloween* (1978) and *Scream* (1996). In David Lynch's *Blue Velvet* (1986), darkness can be found in the beautifully clean neighborhoods of Lumberton, and in Sam Mendes' *American Beauty* (1999) emotional chaos lurks beneath the surface of suburbia.

TRAINS, PLANES, AND AUTOMOBILES

An old lady vanishes on a train, passengers board an airliner that is destined to crash into the sea, Cary Grant embarks on the 20th Century Limited bound for Chicago, a car chase takes place through the San Francisco streets. Hitchcock's films are full of modes of transport and travel. By using transport he knew that he could satisfy an audience's appetite for exotic locations, while at the same time giving his stories forward motion and excitement.

Transport also lends itself to the double chase, which is also the near-perfect form for Hitchcock's suspense stories, where the hero is pursued by both villains and the police simultaneously. Transport and double chases lend themselves very easily for stories of mystery and suspense, and the falsely accused hero crosses huge distances by car, train, or foot as he seeks to clear his name.

When filming inside trains, planes, or cars, Hitchcock always kept the camera inside rather than cutting back to a long shot. In *North by Northwest*, he keeps the camera inside the train, for as he says, "Planting the camera in

Guy and Bruno (Farley Granger and Robert Walker) exchange small talk in the dining car in *Strangers on a Train* (1951).

the countryside to shoot a passing train would merely give us the viewpoint of a cow watching a train go by. I tried to keep the public inside the train. Whenever it went into a curve, we took a long shot from one of the train windows. The way we did that was to put three cameras on the rear platform of the 20th Century Limited, and we went over the exact journey of the film at the same time of the day. One of our cameras was used for the long shots of the train in the curves, while the two others were used for background footage." The effect is to keep the audience more involved with the action by keeping them inside the compartment.

In *Foreign Correspondent*, when the plane is diving down toward the sea because its engines are crippled, Hitchcock keeps the camera inside the cabin, above the shoulders of the two pilots who are trying to pull the plane out of the dive. Between them, through the glass cabin window, we can see the ocean coming closer. And then, without a cut, the plane hits the ocean and the water rushes in, drowning the two men. "That whole thing was done in a single shot without a cut," said Hitchcock. "I had a transparency made of paper, and behind that screen, a water tank. The plane dived, and as soon as the water got close to it, I pressed the button and the water burst through, tearing the screen away. The volume was so great that you never saw the screen."

The same is true for car scenes; once you're in the car you must stay in the car. In *Psycho*, when Marion drives off the main highway looking for a place to say, Hitchcock filmed a mock-up of the car on a soundstage with back projection. He was reluctant to use an exterior shot. Hitch said, "I'm not going to do an external shot. I want to be inside the car when she drives off." So a bicycle wheel with miniature lights was used to replicate the faraway cars on the highway.

During the runaway car scene in *Family Plot*, Hitchcock again keeps the camera inside the car and never shows the exterior after the brake fluid leaks out. He cuts from a mid shot of Blanche and George (Barbara Harris and Bruce Dern) at the wheel, frantically trying to steer the car on the downhill windy road, to their POV of the road, as oncoming traffic, cars and motorcyclists, hurtle past them, before finally coming to a crash in a lay-by upside down. The effect is tense and claustrophobic, keeping the audience inside the car with the characters.

Other directors have used modes of transport for their settings. *Flightplan* (2005), directed by Robert Schwentke, has a strong Hitchcock connection. In particular, it borrows from *The Lady Vanishes* (1938). In each film a female mysteriously disappears — in Hitchcock's version it's an elderly woman on a train, and in *Flightplan* it's a child on an airliner. *Flightplan* also borrows the plot device of using a message written on a window and the hysteria of the central female character as a seeming conspiracy grows around her.

Duncan Jones' *Source Code* (2011) is set on a train, and the very first scene is reminiscent of the encounter between Roger and Eve in *North by Northwest*. Colter Stevens (Jake Gyllenhaal) wakes up on a train opposite a beautiful woman (Michelle Monaghan). The opening music borrows from Bernard Herrmann's famous scores, and the way Jones films the passengers echoes Hitchcock. "I'm not embarrassed to say we borrowed liberally from Hitchcock," says Jones. "It's about an ordinary guy in extraordinary circumstances, sitting on a train across from a mysterious dame, and that's the perfect Hitchcock set-up. So that and the fact that I tried to inject the humor — Hitchcock always had humor running through his films — it felt like this was the perfect opportunity to make a very classic thriller."

USE CONTROLLED LOCATIONS TO INCREASE TENSION

A Manhattan penthouse, a lifeboat at sea, a Greenwich Village apartment overlooking a courtyard of neighbors' windows. Several of Hitchcock's most memorable films are restricted to a single setting to increase the tension, and in doing so, confine the characters to a single space. Hitchcock had a fear of confined spaces, as told by his story of being put in a local jail cell when he was five years old. But he was able to use his fear of confinement in many of his films. Think of the survivors in *Lifeboat*, the murderous villains in *Rope*, and the wheelchair-bound photographer in *Rear Window*. *Lifeboat* was the first film Hitchcock made that was confined to a single setting — he wanted to prove most films are in close shots anyway; "Because I wanted to prove a theory that I had then.

Hitchcock with the cast of *Rope* (1948), which was filmed entirely in a studio-built apartment.

Analyzing the psychological pictures that were being turned out, it seemed to me that visually 80% of the footage was shot in close-ups or semi-close shots. Most likely it wasn't a conscious thing with most directors, but rather an instinctive need to come closer to the action."

Recent films have taken Hitchcock's idea of a single setting and used it to create maximum suspense and tension. Larry Cohen's script for *Phone Booth* (2002) was so high-concept that it went to a bidding war and was sold for six figures. A sleazy PR man (Colin Farrell) is confined to a single setting — trapped in a phone booth — by a crazed sniper (voiced by Kiefer Sutherland). Cohen originally suggested the idea to Hitchcock in the 1960s over lunch, "What about doing a movie in a phone booth since you did one in a lifeboat and one in an apartment looking out the window?" Hitchcock liked the idea, but neither of them could figure out how to do it. Years later,

Cohen came up with the sniper who keeps Farrell trapped inside the booth, and he was able to write the script within a month.

Cohen and director Joel Schumacher cleverly circumnavigated the single setting by having a split screen when Farrell is talking to other people and gave the characters different points of view, all without ever leaving the phone booth. The movie premise was so Hitchcockian that when Steven Spielberg met Cohen at the Oscars, he said, "If Hitchcock were alive, he would have wanted to direct *Phone Booth*."

Interestingly Hitchcock even mentions a phone booth when talking about *Dial M for Murder* (1954), which for the most part takes place in a single living room. "I could just as well have shot the whole film in a telephone booth," he says. "Let's imagine there's a couple in that booth. Their hands are touching, their lips meet, and accidentally one of them leans against the receiver, knocking it off the hook. Now, while they're unaware of it, the phone operator can listen in on their intimate conversation. The drama has taken a step forward. For the audience, looking at the images, it should be the same as reading the opening paragraphs of a novel or hearing the expositional dialogue of the stage play. You might say that a filmmaker can use a telephone booth pretty much in the same way a novelist uses a blank piece of paper."

Other single-setting films include *1408* (2007), *Exam* (2009), and *Buried* (2010). In *Dogville* (2003), directed by Lars von Trier, the action is restricted to a single stage setting, with minimal scenery. Taking place in real time like *Rope,* the suspense remains tight and controlled right down to the final resolution.

FEATURE FAMOUS LANDMARKS

Hitchcock often set action against strong, famous landmarks, such as the United Nations, the Golden Gate

Bridge, and Piccadilly Circus. Often they are combined with his best set pieces. *Blackmail* (1929) features a chase from the dome of the British Museum. The climax of *The Man Who Knew Too Much* (1956) takes place at the Royal Albert Hall in London, *Saboteur* (1942) atop the Statue of Liberty, and *North by Northwest* (1959) on Mount Rushmore. Hitchcock enjoyed placing his characters in great danger in symbols of order.

There are many Hitchcock films, too, which revolve around a city. *Vertigo* showcases San Francisco with major scenes filmed around the city's landmarks. Hitchcock loved San Francisco. He felt it was a very glamorous city, rather like an American Paris, very cosmopolitan, more so that any of the cities he had seen at the time. In *Vertigo*, it becomes a character in itself.

The key factor in the original France-set plot of *Vertigo* was a church tower, and the fact that the church had to be a place of some visual interest and remote so that the murder could be committed with comfort. The problem was transferring the story from France to America, as there aren't the old churches as there are in France, except for the old missions in California. Hitchcock, who had a house near Santa Cruz, knew of San Juan Baptiste Mission, which had originally had a short tower. For the purposes of the film, a tower was matte-printed on. Geographically the mission worked too, because it was near San Francisco, which was why it was chosen. San Francisco is such a beautiful city and its vertiginous hills evoke the theme of the film as well. *The Birds* also starts in San Francisco, with Melanie Daniels crossing Union Square on her way to a pet shop. Other Hitchcock-inspired movies set in San Francisco include *Pacific Heights* (1990), *Final Analysis* (1992), and *Basic Instinct* (1992).

Martin Scorsese's *Shutter Island* (2010) abounds in Hitchcock references, including a very high building sequence that is reminiscent of *Vertigo,* a shower scene like *Psycho*, and a rock face climb that echoes *North by Northwest.*

MAKE YOUR SETS REALISTIC

Hitchcock always strived to make his sets and backgrounds as realistic as he could for his movies. Even though his actors seem to be detached from the background in many of his films, because of Hitch's fondness for using back projection and preference for shooting inside a studio rather than location, he kept the background designs realistic, clear, sharp, and idealized. The effect was to make his often fantastic stories as vivid as possible, so that many of his films take on the form of dreams.

After the set is painted, the set dresser comes on. When Hitchcock was working in the studio, he said that he used to have problems with the set dressers. They were the people who go and buy furniture and dress the set up, whereas Hitch believed they should be more of a writer and know about the character of an individual. He was also very concerned about the authenticity of settings and furnishings. When he couldn't shoot in the actual settings such as the delegates' lounge of the United Nations in *North by Northwest*, he and his assistant disguised themselves as tourists and took photographs, and then created the lounge on a soundstage. In *Topaz*, to reproduce the interiors of the Hotel Harlem, photographs and postcards from the period were used when Fidel Castro had stayed at the hotel.

Think of some iconic sets in Hitchcock's films — the mansion of the three and a half fingered man in *The 39 Steps*, the bell tower and the art gallery in *Vertigo*, the motel and the Bates house in *Psycho*, and the Frank Lloyd Wright house in *North by Northwest*. Eva Marie Saint remembers, "I loved that set. It was stylish and modern. It really felt like a house and had a whole second floor for climbing." The shower stall in *Psycho* was actually built in sections 12' x 12' across, so it could be partly disassembled, allowing for all the camera set-ups. In *Rear Window*, Hitchcock had an entire apartment building with a courtyard mocked up so that each apartment window facing the courtyard functioned like a miniature movie screen, revealing its own resident's small story.

Houses often play a key role in Hitchcock's films and are characters in themselves. In *Rebecca*, Manderley is the name of the imposing house that Maxim de Winter (Laurence Olivier) and his new wife Mrs. de Winter (Joan Fontaine) live in, and even features in the film's famous opening line: "Last night I dreamt I went to Manderley again." *Rebecca* could be called the story of a house. Hitchcock said, "The house had no geographical place, it was separated, she went up a driveway and that was it." You get an impression of the village from the inquest scene, but all the action takes place inside the house, which adds to the claustrophobic feel as the housekeeper Mrs. Danvers (Judith Anderson) terrorizes the new wife.

The gothic gingerbread house in *Psycho* also contributes immensely to the film's spooky feel of Victorian horror and the sense of desolation evoked by its inspiration from Edward Hopper's paintings. This is played to the maximum when Lila explores the house in search of Mrs. Bates. Something of that same isolated element comes into play for the house in *The Birds*. "I had the instinct, I must keep that house alone, to make sure the fear that the house has no support, like a next door neighbor or another building," said Hitchcock.

"What I learned from Hitch, I carried out my same theme of making sets look like the people that lived there," said Henry Bumstead, the art designer for *Vertigo*. "He liked to see what people do in that room." Scottie Ferguson was an ex-cop and at the time Bumstead was a stamp collector, so he made Scottie one too — he had that in one part of the set. Hitch loved to see those things because it showed that the designer was thinking and trying to make that character a real person.

Actress Karin Dor remembers that *Topaz* was shooting in Florida to double as Cuba, which of course was off-limits for American film crews. Palm trees that were native to Cuba were shipped to the set to make the setting more authentic. Hitchcock also had an eye for detail and continuity. Karin remembers a scene when she is having breakfast with her French lover, played by Frederick Stafford; "We couldn't finish the scene, and the next day they had torn down some decoration because there were visitors on the set. We had great continuity people, and when we resumed filming Hitchcock said to them, 'I want to see everything exactly the same way as before.' He let us rehearse and then the cameraman said he was ready to shoot. Hitch said 'Well I'm not ready; something is not right on the table.' I looked at my plate, and there was the same amount of scrambled eggs, and the fork was in the same place. I looked at the liquor and it was the same amount left in the glass. He let all of us, including those continuity men, sweat. Then he told us what was missing — the print of my lipstick on my drinking glass. You couldn't see it, but Hitch saw it."

USE COLOR SPARINGLY

"I prefer color because there is plenty to dramatize in color by not using color until you need it dramatically." — *Alfred Hitchcock*

Hitchcock was a master of color and often compared his technique to that of a painter. Some of his best color films include *Vertigo*, *Marnie*, and *Topaz*. His favorite color was green, and he wanted his actresses to wear it, such as Grace Kelly's green suit in *Rear Window* and Tippi Hedren's chic outfit in *The Birds*. In *Vertigo*, the color green symbolizes mystery and later reincarnation when Madeleine seemingly appears from the dead. When Scottie initially follows her, she drives a green car. Even after Madeleine has seemingly committed suicide, Scottie first spots Judy wearing a green dress, linking her to Madeleine by the association with green.

As Hitchcock said, "I like color. It's true that I filmed *Psycho* in black and white to avoid showing red blood in the killing of Janet Leigh in the shower. On the other hand, since color pictures, we have problems with the decors. Violent contrast — for instance, extravagant luxury or abject poverty — can be expressed with precision and clarity on the screen. However, if we wish to show an average apartment, it is difficult to create a realistic decor because of the risk of the lack of precision."

For Hitchcock, color should start with the nearest equivalent to black and white, but color "should be no different from the voice which starts muted and finally arrives at a scream." For example, if you take a country scene in the winter, with a gray mist to it, just fields and bare trees, nothing in bright color, that's just as effective as black and white because you can feel the coldness from the bleak color. In a color film, if you want to reduce a scene to black and white, you can use nothing but grays. Hitchcock didn't like bright colors unless the story says "there goes a girl in a red dress," and he never used poster colors.

These garish colors were never used on the screen except for effect. One advantage of color is that it gives you more immediate shades. Just imagine you are filming in a company director's office, and the directors are all in dark clothes and white collars. Suddenly the chairman's wife comes in, wearing a red hat. She takes the attention of the audience at once, just because of that one note of color. Color is part of the structure. In other words, you restrain color and bring it in when it's necessary. The color psychology is fairly standard. While blue and gray are cool colors, orange and apricot are warm, receptive colors.

Some filmmakers believe that black and white movies create better mood for a film, but Hitchcock believed the same could be true for color films. "I think color should be reduced and desaturated down so that the only color left on screen is the fresh color of the face...You can always control color by desaturation," he said. In *Torn Curtain*, after the action moves from Copenhagen the color scheme is beige and gray. No more color occurs after that. The corridor in the Berlin hotel is gray except for a red fire extinguisher.

COSTUME FOR CHARACTER

Costume together with color plays an essential role in Hitchcock's films. He would sit down with the wardrobe supervisor to create the look of the picture, often in conjunction with the production designer. This attention to the costume helped the actors visualize their characters.

Hitchcock forged a lasting collaboration with Edith Head, the famed costume designer, and it's been described as a match made in heaven. Head designed the costumes for eleven of his films, from *Notorious* (1946) through *Family Plot* (1976), and she favored elegant simplicity, typified by Ingrid Bergman's beautiful monochrome look in *Notorious* of blacks, grays, and whites. Bergman's "notorious" Alicia Huberman wears white on her first date with Alex Sebastian (Claude Rains), wears black when she spies on him, and in her first scene with T.R. Devlin (Cary Grant) is wearing black and white stripes to show her ambiguity.

As Kim Novak says about working with Hitchcock on *Vertigo*, "He was very definite about every detail on how you looked. It was very important, the look of the character. He gave me more freedom in playing Judy than Madeleine. That was intentional on his part to make me feel more comfortable in the role. He allowed me to choose the clothes that Judy wore and was very agreeable. I had a shoe fetish at the time. I didn't like wearing the dark shoes of Madeleine. So Hitchcock said what would you like to use for Judy? I said my own skin color, neutral, so he gave me the choice on that. Being in the shoes that belonged to you was a wise decision on Hitch's part. In her head, Judy was so mixed up, so wearing those neutral shoes, she felt like a piece of the earth like her Kansas background."

The black shoes that Novak wore as Madeleine, on the other hand, were very uncomfortable. That worked for her to get into character. "It made me feel out of place," Novak says. "She was having to pretend all the time, and be something that she wasn't, [so] that was part of helping me in the role."

Costume also played an important role in *Psycho*. Helen Colvig, the film's costume designer, remembers, "I had to buy the lingerie for Janet Leigh as Hitchcock did not want anything that seemed to be custom made. He said 'I don't want anything fancy, I want something practical that women wear every day.' So I chose the Olga bra. The style is very practical…He wanted the authenticity and demanded having women dressed as ordinary working girls. I respected that. A lot of time the actress has the last word. But Hitchcock was the last word. I was there when Janet Leigh said she'd like to have the lingerie made to order, but he said no, he wanted it off the rack. Later when Marion changes from a white bra to a black bra, he wanted the change to show that she was not the goody two shoes that she was in the office."

Hitchcock was extremely thorough in his preparation. Helen Colvig praises Hitchcock, saying, "He was so on the mark with everything, all the little things mattered to him." Today she recommends that costume designers listen closely to what the director or producer envision for the best collaborative results.

The result of showing Janet Leigh in off-the-rack underwear was that many ordinary American women in the audience related to her character. As George Sluizer, the director of *The Vanishing* (1988), says "The underwear which Janet Leigh wore in *Psycho* had, according to Hitchcock, to be identifiable to as many women as possible, to suck them as deep as he could into the plot — an important detail that I remembered when I wanted the audience to identify with characters in my films." So costuming can have an important psychological effect upon your audience.

The careful color coordination of *Marnie* and *Topaz* is reflected in the costume design. Marnie tends to wear greens, browns, and yellows, which act as camouflage, and has an aversion to red, which goes back to a trauma in her childhood. Hitchcock rarely used red, except to make a bold statement. During the filming of *Topaz*, Hitch specifically asked for Karin Dor, playing Juanita de Cordoba, to be dressed in red in her first scene. "Edith Head had designed a beautiful lavender dress for me," remembers Karin, "but Hitchcock said no, I want her to be in red. So Edith and her staff had to work all night to make me the beautiful red dress. Hitchcock wanted the scene to be passionate."

Knowing how carefully Hitchcock planned his films, the red in Juanita's dress links her with Communism, as she is first seen with Ricco Parra, her Cuban lover. But when she is with her French lover, her allegiances shift and she wears yellow. Yellow is very much identified with the French in *Topaz*, such as the French spy Dubois, played by Roscoe Lee Browne, who wears a yellow smock in the flower shop, and the yellow floral motifs that occur throughout the film.

And it's not just the women who received attention from Hitchcock's careful coordination of color and wardrobe. *North by Northwest* has been described as being a film about Cary Grant's suit, and the Saville Row tailored gray suit he wears has been dubbed as "the best suit in film history." And it shows contrast. Grant standing in that prairie wasteland in a business suit made a visual statement that a tweed jacket and slacks never would have. "There is a certain amount of value to be got from what one might term visual incongruity," said Hitch.

Grant's incongruous dress is similar to when sophisticated Melanie Daniels (Tippi Hedren) arrives to the sleepy town of Bodega Bay driving an Aston Martin convertible in *The Birds*. She hires a boat and crosses the bay in her fur coat, carrying a birdcage. It's very surrealistic and she presents a striking contrast to her background. As Hitchcock said, "I think, for example, the girl getting into a boat with two birds in a cage, wearing a mink coat in an outboard, is kind of ridiculous, you see. But that again is counterpointing. A visual counterpoint to what would normally happen."

One of the reasons Hitchcock's films hold up so well over time and don't appear to date is his sense of classicism, reflected in his costume design. Even a picture like *Rebecca*, from 1940, still seems fresh and contemporary in its feel. That's because of the sense of classicism that Hitchcock brought to his films.

Eva Marie Saint remembers an incident during the filming of *North by Northwest* that shows Hitchcock's awareness of classicism. Extras for a scene had shown up wearing shift dresses without a waistline or a belt. Hitchcock sent them all home, Saint remembers, "Because that particular fashion was 'in' fashion and it would date the film...he says he was very meticulous and had definite ideas about what you wore."

Similarly, in *Frenzy*, which was shot in England in 1971, during the filming of a street scene with two young women in micro skirts, Hitchcock asked for the scene to be reshot with the women in less trendy clothing so that the film wouldn't date, as so many from that period later proved to do.

One director who understands very well Hitchcock's sense of classicism is the American designer and director Tom Ford. In his film *A Single Man* (2009) the Hitchcock influence is obvious from the beginning, from a wall backdrop of Janet Leigh's eyes in *Psycho* to a score that evokes Bernard Herrmann. "Hitchcock is one of my favorite directors. Everything in his movies is absolutely stylized and I'm about exaggerated, enhanced reality," says Ford. "Even if I end up doing something unstylish, it will be stylishly unstylish. So it wasn't that I set out to make a stylish film, it was more like, 'Let's move that clock slightly, that painting is horrible, he would never have had that.'"

Like Hitchcock, Tom Ford knows his characters inside out. He used binders of visual references for each character and knew what cologne his main character wore; he knew that his stationery was from Smythson's, and put Saville Row labels in his jackets. By paying attention to the detail of his character's dress he was able to flesh out who they were and how they behaved. So if you want your movie not to date, think classic — elegant, simple, and long-lasting.

Director Pedro Almodóvar has also been inspired by Hitchcock, especially *Vertigo,* and Hitchcock's sense of costume and color is evident in many of Almodóvar's films, including *Volver* (2006) and *The Skin I Live In* (2011). As Almodóvar says, "In *Vertigo*, when James Stewart tries to transform Kim Novak by changing her hairstyle and buying her a new wardrobe, he's basically creating the woman of his dreams. In a way, he's doing exactly what a director does when he's working with an actress to create a character. It reminds me of working with Penélope Cruz, deciding how she would wear her hair, trying on wigs and different dresses, until we got what I wanted."

STORYBOARD YOUR FILM

"I am a puritan and a believer in the visuals." — *Alfred Hitchcock*

Storyboards are often a way of getting a sense of how an idea will work, before putting it down on film or tape. They consist of a series of images, like the panels of a comic strip that give you an idea of how to compose different scenes. Both the sequences in front of the camera and the movements of the camera itself can be sketched out, like in a comic strip.

Hitchcock is probably more famous for storyboarding than any other director. He used elaborate boards to refine his vision, ensuring that his intention was translated to the screen for his collaborators, long before the shooting actually began. Often he famously boasted that he rarely looked through the camera viewfinder on the set, since it was merely a photographic equivalent of a storyboard that had been finalized earlier.

Pat Hitchcock, his daughter, remembers, "He would take the finished screenplay and sit in his office with a piece of paper, a pad, with three rectangles on and draw every single shot in the movie. Then he would get the cameraman in and show him what the movie looked like. So when he got on the set, he said he had already made the film. That's what was so great about working with him, because then he could devote all his attention to the actors."

Hitchcock was so meticulous that he considered this phase in the production — the drawing of storyboards — to be the actual process of making the film. For him

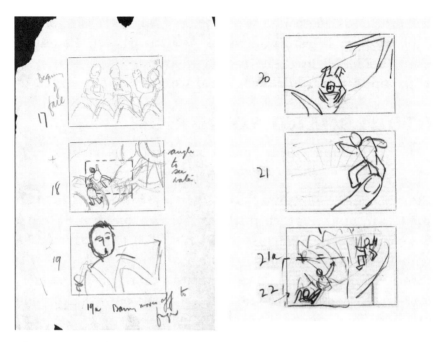

Hitchcock's hand-drawn storyboards for *Saboteur* (1942).

shooting the film was a "necessary evil," while the planning of the storyboards was where most of the creative work took place.

When Hitchcock was making *Saboteur* in 1942, he hand-sketched the famous Statue of Liberty scene where Norman Lloyd, playing the villain, is hanging off the statue and is being held by the sleeve by the hero, played by Robert Cummings. Lloyd remembers Hitchcock showing him the storyboards for that scene; "I had just come from the New York theatre and I didn't know anything about filmmaking. Hitch asked me, 'Would you like to see the Statue of Liberty scene?' And I said, 'But we haven't shot it yet!' So Hitch laid it out in a scroll-like affair, all the storyboards he had done. It was like a Biblical scroll."

Lucinda Barrett, who plays a small part in *The Wrong Man* as one of the office workers who mistakenly identifies "the wrong man," remembers, "Hitchcock showed me all the storyboards for the movie, cut by cut, scene by scene. He made it clear that he didn't deviate from the storyboards, even the smallest details, such as the slant of a window shade at a certain level. The storyboards were in pages in a book, all hand-drawn and illustrated."

Storyboards not only determine exactly what the shot will look like, they can even decide what kind of lens is used. Production for Hitchcock, then, was simply a matter of creating live versions of the storyboards he'd already made. Storyboards can describe the size of the shot, whether it's a medium or a tight close-up, whether the camera pulls back and pans to the right as the character walks toward the door, whether it tilts slightly down and shoots through the open doorway.

As Hitchcock started his profession as an art director, he would often storyboard himself, as the sketches for *Saboteur* show. On *Psycho*, Marshall Schlom, the script supervisor remembers, "The cameraman would line up the shot, I carried a piece of paper around with me, and Hitchcock would draw a frame line and show the cameraman sketches of what he wanted to do. I learned so much from these pieces of papers, because I listened to him describe what he wanted to do." But the finer, more elaborate work conceived for the bulk of his films was done by other specialists, such as Robert Boyle and Harold Michelson. In storyboarding a script for a Hitchcock film, an illustrator was told what pictures to be put on the boards by the script and through conferences with the director. The screenwriter would also participate in what is going to appear on that storyboard, because even without the storyboard the script describes exactly what is going to be on the screen. That was the way Hitchcock liked to work.

Their usual way of working together began with meetings early in the production schedule to go over each scene. Hitchcock might furnish rough thumbnail sketches to elaborate a sequence, but this process was also intended to allow his creative team to draw on each other's ideas. From these meetings, a general plan was devised for each scene, some more detailed than others.

Only rarely would an entire film be storyboarded, such as *The Birds*, which required various departments to work together to create the complicated special effects required for the movie. Storyboards were mainly done for key sequences that required lots of cuts, such as the shower scene in *Psycho* and the car chase in *Family Plot*.

According to Robert Boyle, during the design of *North by Northwest*, "For certain sequences like Mount Rushmore or Vandamm's house, we did storyboards, but we were moving so fast on that production that we didn't have time to do them for the crop-duster sequence." The famous crop-duster storyboard was drawn later for publicity purposes, but most of the time storyboards were drawn before filming started.

STORYBOARDING BEYOND HITCHCOCK: PRE-VISUALIZATION

Today the storyboard equivalent is called "pre-visualization." Anything that helps actors imagine what is being shot is called "pre-viz" and it's a collaborative process that generates preliminary versions of shots or sequences, predominantly using 3D animation tools and a virtual environment. Pre-viz enables filmmakers to visually explore creative ideas, plan technical solutions, and communicate a shared vision to all members of the production team. A director can see the story beats and how the flow is taking place.

Without pre-viz Spielberg's elaborate and exciting action sequences would not have the same flair and sophistication as Hitchcock's. During the production of *Raiders of the Lost Ark* (1981), for instance, Spielberg used a model of the Nazi airfield in order to plan the sequence where Indiana Jones fights under the flying wing. For the second *Star Wars* trilogy, George Lucas pre-visualized his scenes before they were shot to create the characters and alien worlds.

Ridley Scott used storyboards for his films such as *Alien* (1979), *Blade Runner* (1982), and *Gladiator* (2000), and calls the storyboard the "first look of the film. You can go down the board and see the film." Hitchcock loved keeping up with technology and would have surely embraced all the pre-visualization and technology that is taking place in today's movies.

EXERCISES

1. Write down one location for your film. Let's say it's a shopping mall or a store like Bed, Bath and Beyond. What can you do to make the location a dramatic element in your plot? What if a flash mob move into the space where your romantic man and woman have just begun to argue?

2. Is your movie exciting and full of motion? How can transport move your story forward in an interesting way?

3. Think of some famous landmarks near where you story is set. Can you incorporate them into the plot to make it more suspenseful and visually interesting?

4. Take a key scene in your movie script. Visualize what the actors are wearing and how color can enhance the story. What does it say about your characters?

5. Then with the same characters change the costume dramatically. What is the effect upon the scene? What if a deadly villain shows up in black (a cliché) and then in the next scene shows up in white or a bright shirt. What has happened to the mood?

6. Get a DVD of your favorite movie; sit down in front of the monitor, with a pencil and paper. Now find your

favorite scene in the movie. Now freeze the frame on the first shot of the sequence and draw a still representation of that image. Remember, storyboards don't have to be full of detail. Even simple stick figures, though they're not very detailed, can effectively communicate the way the shot will look.

Key Hitchcock films to watch

Saboteur (1942)
Vertigo (1958)
North by Northwest (1959)
Marnie (1964)
Topaz (1969)

Other directors' films to watch

Alien (1979)
Raiders of the Lost Ark (1981)
Phone Booth (2002)
Flightplan (2005)
A Single Man (2009)

Further reading

Hitchcock at Work (2000) by Bill Krohn

CHAPTER FOUR

WORKING WITH ACTORS

> *"Well, first and foremost, what I look for in talent, especially when we are in the area of the purely cinematic, is the mobility of the face. In other words, expression. The register of expression. Especially in subjective treatment it's a very vital thing you see... The reaction."* — *Alfred Hitchcock*

The great stars in a Hitchcock film are wonderful to look at. Heroes have beautiful profiles, wavy hair, and handsome flesh. Heroines are blonde, poised, and elegant. There's the luminous beauty of Ingrid Bergman in *Notorious*, the cool perfection of Grace Kelly in *To Catch a Thief*, the everyman affability of James Stewart in *Rear Window*, and the self-effacing charm, grace, and athleticism of Cary Grant in *North by Northwest*.

Hitchcock worked with many great stars of the day, including Carole Lombard, Laurence Olivier, Tallulah

Alfred Hitchcock
with Cary Grant, the
man he wanted to
be — handsome, sexy,
sophisticated.

Bankhead, Ray Milland, James Mason, Montgomery Clift, Henry Fonda, Marlene Dietrich, Doris Day, Kim Novak, Sean Connery, Julie Andrews, and Paul Newman. When given the choice, however, he preferred to work with stars from whom he knew what to expect, which is why so many actors appeared in his films again and again. Cary Grant and James Stewart appeared in four films apiece for the director, and Ingrid Bergman and Grace Kelly each appeared in three. Other repeat performers include Gregory Peck, Charles Laughton, Joan Fontaine, Robert Cummings, Joseph Cotten, Michael Wilding, John Forsythe, Farley Granger, Vera Miles, and Tippi Hedren. Character actor Leo G. Carroll appeared in six Hitchcock films, more than anyone other than Hitch himself (in cameo).

CASTING

"I've always said that Walt Disney has the right idea. His actors are made of paper. When he doesn't like them, he can tear them up."
— *Alfred Hitchcock*

Hitchcock said that 75% of directing is casting and he often waded through pages of casting suggestions and watched dozens of films in his private screening room. With a professional eye he chose his actors carefully to fit the part that he imagined, often working closely with the writer. Think of the great performances in a Hitchcock film and how the casting enhances them. What would *Notorious* be like without Ingrid Bergman, Cary Grant, and Claude Rains? Or *Rear Window* without James Stewart, Grace Kelly, Thelma Ritter, and Raymond Burr? Or *Psycho* without Anthony Perkins and Janet Leigh?

If you're lucky enough to have a star like Cary Grant in your movie, you have an immediate advantage. As well as playing the character of Roger Thornhill, a suave and sophisticated advertising exec on Madison Avenue, Grant brings his own personality to the part in a film like *North by Northwest*. Despite the character being rather shallow — he steals a cab from another guy by falsely explaining that his secretary is pregnant — the audience immediately roots for him and identifies with his character, chiefly because he is played by Cary Grant. That's the value of casting a star.

AVOID THE CLICHÉ IN YOUR CHARACTERS

To avoid the cliché in your films, do the exact opposite of what the audience expects in a movie. Keep the audience engaged, and asking what will happen next. Surprise them both conceptually and visually. Make the dumb blondes smart blondes, criminals should be attractive, and the old lady could be a spy. They should have unexpected personalities, making decisions on a whim rather than what previous buildup would suggest. These sorts of ironic characters make them more realistic to the audience, and ripe for something to happen to them.

"Unfortunately, when you're dealing with melodrama, you mustn't let the characters take them where they want to go, they must come where you want to go," said Hitchcock. "It's an inverted process, it's a bastard form of storytelling. You lay out your story and then you put the characters in afterwards. That's why you don't get good characterization if there isn't time. And in case they may not want to go."

In *Frenzy* the casting director kept sending barmaids who were blonde and bosomy for the role of Babs the Cockney barmaid, but Hitchcock cast against type and hired Anna Massey, who was more of a character actress. The same is true for Jean Marsh, who played Monica the secretary. "When he cast you, he presumed you could do it," says Jean. Quite a lot of film actors are better when they are doing nothing except essentially being themselves.

One of the most vivid characters in *Torn Curtain* is Gromek, played by the German actor Wolfgang Kieling. Gromek talks nostalgically about living in New York, and even though he is the heavy in this movie, he comes across as a three-dimensional character. "I think Gromek was created as all the characters were, as a human being," said Hitchcock. "Other films seemed to make communists granite-faced individuals and humorless, which I don't believe. So all the German characters were created as human beings with a family. This was setting him up. I laid down the rules that no-one could speak English unless they were either educated, a senior official, or had been in America." The result was one of the most memorable character parts in Hitchcock's films.

AUDIENCE IDENTIFICATION

"I've learned from experience that whenever the hero isn't portrayed by a star, the whole picture suffers." — Alfred Hitchcock

Making an audience identify with the character was very important for Hitchcock when he was casting. He knew that you get more suspense out of an audience if they worry about a star than if they were watching an unknown actor. An audience is more likely to get the shakes at the thought of James Stewart or Cary Grant being killed, rather than someone unknown. If you walk through the streets and see an unknown man lying there after being hit by a car, you would think "poor fellow." But if you take a double-look and he's your brother, then it's a very different emotion. For Hitchcock that is one very important aspect of suspense and identification that boils down to "Are you 100% anxious about that particular star?"

Today's action thrillers heavily depend on star charisma for their box office success. Casting is especially important in movies such as the *Bourne* films with Matt Damon, the Jason Statham movies, or *Source Code* with Jake Gyllenhaal, where the audience becomes involved in the adventures of the hero, especially when his life is in danger. The bigger the star, such as Tom Cruise in the *Mission: Impossible* films, the bigger the audience identification. The lesser-known the performer, the lesser the audience's interest is likely to be.

USE CLOSE-UPS

Hitchcock knew about the magnetic power of stars, and let his camera linger on the porcelain beauty of Grace Kelly and the handsome visage of Cary Grant for audience gratification. He allowed the charisma and charm of his biggest stars to woo the audience. Actors were hired because he believed they could play the role and for their star quality.

A good way to make your actors and characters stand out is by photographing them in big close-ups and capturing their reactions so that the audience will identify with them. Hitchcock liked to film his stars close-up so you could admire their physique and empathize with their emotions. He adored Ingrid Bergman and in *Notorious* films her beautiful face in a series of big close-ups. When Alicia (Bergman) realizes that Alex (Claude Rains) and his mother are trying to poison her, the audience feels empathy for her and the trapped situation she is in. "I have a weakness for *Notorious* because of Ingrid Bergman's face," said director Theo Angelopoulos. And Hitchcock introduced Grace Kelly's character in big close-ups in *Rear Window* as she approaches and kisses a sleeping Jeffries (James Stewart). It's an enthralling way to present Kelly, who is the beautiful blonde heroine of the film.

Hitchcock felt that it was important to give the audience every chance to know and understand the characters they are looking at. This is all part of giving the audience information, so that they could anticipate what's coming up and grasp what's happening. He achieved this not so much through camera techniques, but by casting actors who knew how to express a mood or intention with a change of expression or the slightest gesture. For Hitchcock, understatement was priceless, and the best actors were those who can be effective even when they are not doing anything.

Alec McCowen remembers how Hitchcock asked him not to rush his entrance when he first appears at the scene of the murder in *Frenzy*, because he wanted the audience to get used to him, his appearance and voice, in his part as the police inspector who eventually captures the real killer. A director can also help an actor by taking care of his physical positions and blocking his movements.

Imagine you have a man in a room chatting to a friend, and then his enemy walks through the front door. At first the man is smiling and then he sees his enemy walk in. It's easier for that actor to show feelings of shock, expressed by the sudden vanishing of that smile, than it is if he starts registering theatrical terror. This is effective contrast and is more true to life and believable.

LESS IS MORE

"I would almost say that the best screen actor is the man who can do nothing extremely well." — Alfred Hitchcock

Hitchcock liked actors whose faces could register expression, which is why he used James Stewart and Cary Grant again and again. "I don't direct them. I talk to them and explain to them what the scene is, what its purpose is, why they are doing certain things — because they relate to the story — not to the scene," says Hitch. The whole scene relates to the story, but that little look does this or that for the story."

At the same time he had trouble with actors who tended to register more expression than he wanted. As Hitchcock recounts to Kim Novak on the set of *Vertigo*, "You have got a lot of expression in your face. Don't want any of it. I only want on your face what we want to tell to the audience — what you are thinking....If you put a lot of redundant expressions on your face, it's like taking a piece of paper and scribbling all over it — full of scribble, the whole piece of paper. You want to write a sentence for somebody to read. They can't read it — too much scribble on the face. Much easier to read if the piece of paper is blank. That's what your face ought to be when we need the expression."

Often Hitchcock said that his best actors did "nothing" very well. He liked their faces to be a blank canvas on which he could let his camera linger. This is why he sometimes took on the challenge of hiring less-experienced performers, such as Tippi Hedren, and literally molded their faces to the required expression, because they had nothing to unlearn. The best Hitchcock actor had to submit himself or herself to his camera and behave quietly and naturally. His camera would then add the expression, accent, and emphasis.

In *The Birds*, Hitchcock boasts that there is not one redundant expression on Tippi Hedren's face. "Every expression makes a point. Even the slight nuance of a smile when she says, 'What can I do for you, sir?' One look says, 'I'm going to play a gag on him.' That's the economy of it." Diane Baker says that while filming *Marnie*, Hitchcock literally molded the look he wanted on her face when her character is spying through the bedroom window as Mark and Marnie are talking outside the front door.

WHEN STARS DON'T SHINE

Occasionally there were a few misfires of casting in Hitchcock's films, such as Paul Newman and Julie Andrews playing improbable scientists in *Torn Curtain*; but more often than not, this was because Hitchcock was unable to get his original choice or because those stars were imposed on him by the studio. He couldn't have anticipated the impact that Kim Novak would have on the power of *Vertigo*, however, as he had originally wanted Vera Miles for the role and was resistant to Novak from the start. Sometimes things work out.

Despite his director status, Hitchcock often was unable to get the stars he wanted, which compromised the integrity of the movie. For Hitchcock *Saboteur* was not a successful picture "Because I don't think [Robert] Cummings was right. He was too undramatic. He has what I call a comedy face, and half the time you don't believe the situations. Think of the difference between that and Robert Donat in *The 39 Steps*." In fact all the casting of *Saboteur* was wrong for Hitch, as the studio cast Priscilla Lane as the heroine without any consultation with him. He had wanted Barbara Stanwyck for the role. "The casting of the heavy Otto Kruger was also a mess to me," said Hitchcock, who had a firm concept of fascists in America and wanted Harry Carey as a rich rancher. He had similar casting problems with *Foreign Correspondent*; Hitchcock wanted Gary Cooper to play the central role, but was given Joel McCrae.

Sometimes casting a well-known star can hinder your movie and work against your aspirations and intentions. In *The Lodger* (1927), Hitchcock cast matinee idol Ivor Novello as the sinister man who rents a room in a London household. The film was adapted from a 1913 novel by Mrs. Belloc Lowndes and was loosely based on the Jack the Ripper murders. But the casting of Novello forced Hitchcock to change the plot. Novello was a big star in England at the time, and he was often associated with being the romantic hero in a film, so it was difficult for the audience to believe in him as a serial killer. Hitchcock had to compromise and show that he wasn't a murderer after all, by proving his innocence at the end. "So obviously putting that kind of actor into those sort of films is a mistake because you have to compromise," he said.

This is the down side of the "star system." Hitchcock ran into the same problem again when he made *Suspicion* (1941) with Cary Grant. Grant was the biggest star of his day and a romantic hero, most often cast in romantic comedies. Yet in *Suspicion*, Grant was cast against type as a shifty husband whose wife (Joan Fontaine) is convinced is a murderer. Hitch intended to film an ending that showed that the wife was correct — Grant's character really was a killer — and devised a scene where the wife writes a letter to her mother describing her suspicions. When the husband ultimately brings his wife a glass of poisoned milk to drink, she asks him to post the letter. She writes, "Dear Mother, I'm desperately in love with him, but I don't want to live because he's a killer. Though I'd rather die, I think society should be protected from him." Then she drinks the milk and dies. The last shot is of the cheery, whistling husband popping the letter in the mailbox — unknowingly sealing his own fate.

Unfortunately that subversive ending was never allowed, with Hitchcock instead being forced to film an ending where it's shown that the husband is proven not to be a murderer and that the suspicions were all in the wife's neurotic head. It would have been brave and pioneering for Hitchcock in 1941 to cast Cary Grant as a wife murderer, but unfortunately the studio and star system prevented him from doing so.

Cary Grant carrying a suspect glass of milk in *Suspicion* (1941). Hitchcock was faced with the problem of portraying a major star as a possible murderer.

KILL OFF YOUR MAIN STAR

You've got the biggest star that your movie's budget can afford. What are you going to do? Kill your star off in the first act! In 1960, that's precisely what Hitchcock did in *Psycho*, an act that proved to be one of the biggest game-changers in movie history. Just over 40 minutes into the film, Hitch kills off the film's biggest star, Janet Leigh. "All the audience went 'Arggghhhh!,'" said Leigh. "It's not possible to kill off the leading lady not even half-way through the picture. But that's what Hitchcock did because he was so smart!"

The audience would have no reason to anticipate that Leigh would die so early in the film, so that's where playing with casting can be very effective. The entire first half of *Psycho* is a red herring designed to throw the audience off balance. It was screenwriter Joseph Stefano who came up with the idea of starting the film with the story of a secretary, Marion Crane, who steals $40,000 from her employee. Hitchcock immediately said, "We can get a star." Because of the star casting, for 40 minutes the audience thinks the movie is about a woman who's a thief. Until she gets into the shower at the Bates Motel, and the entire story changes.

Hitchcock was smart because he also cast against type. If the suits were casting the picture, they would have put a lesser actress in the first act, because she is dispensable. They would have given Janet Leigh the second part of Lila Crane, Marion's sister, who survives until the end of the movie. For Hitchcock that was idiot thinking, because the whole point is to kill off the star, which makes it so unexpected — and shows how casting can be a very important part of suspense.

After Marion is killed, Marion's sister Lila (Vera Miles) and boyfriend Sam (John Gavin) investigate her disapperance. But Hitchcock made sure that there is no

In *Psycho* (1960), Hitchcock caused a sensation by killing off Janet Leigh's character less than halfway through the movie.

identification with these secondary characters and that there's no hint of love interest between them. With only 48 minutes left in the movie, there wasn't any time to develop them and there was no need to. The characters of Sam and Lila become an extension of the audience, leading the viewer through the final part of the picture, which is the story of Norman Bates and his mother.

Killing off your main star before you reach the halfway point of your movie is sure to provide your audience with some shocks, and it's a ploy that has been imitated by many other directors. In Wes Craven's *Scream* (1996), the director killed off star Drew Barrymore in the first ten minutes; "I found *Psycho* fascinating to watch, because of how Hitchcock was deconstructing expectations and building up a central character and then killing her before he was supposed to. He was totally in command

and completely free to break the rules. And obviously *Scream* began like that."

In *To Live and Die in L.A.* (1985), director William Friedkin kills off Willem Dafoe, the star of the movie, 20 minutes before the end. Friedkin says he too borrowed this from *Psycho*. "In *Psycho*, you think for the first 35 minutes of the film that you're watching a story about a woman who has embezzled some money. And a half an hour later, she's dead; she's not in the movie anymore. He completely took away your stability by killing the star."

"It's always good to kill movie stars," says Steven Soderbergh, director of the deadly virus thriller *Contagion* (2011). "I think that the two most important things that have happened to that aspect of movies in the last 50 years are Hitchcock killing off Janet Leigh in a way that nobody had ever dreamed of doing — taking his heroine and killing her off after 40 minutes — and Mike Nichols casting Dustin Hoffman in *The Graduate*. That changed everything."

Soderbergh's thriller *Contagion* is filled with an all-star cast, including Gwyneth Paltrow, Kate Winslet, Laurence Fishburne, and Matt Damon. Ten minutes into the movie Gwyneth Paltrow's character dies. This is a clear signal to the audience that nobody is safe. Some of his stars will live, and some of his stars will die, and the audience is kept hooked to the end, to see who ultimately survives.

Eli Roth, the director of *Cabin Fever* (2002) and *Hostel* (2005) has also been hugely influenced by Hitchcock. In *Hostel*, he says, "I stole the protagonist switch from *Psycho*. Let's just take a guy, make him the main charac-ter, say 'This is our star, this is his story,' then just kill him off halfway through. Now you're stuck in a strange country, you don't know the language, you don't know the people, there's the fear of the police. Which Hitchcock had a real fear of police, that's certainly in there. We were going for a Hitchcock style, and that's really our nod to Hitchcock and *Psycho* and *North by Northwest*."

SOLID HEROES

Nora Ephron, the director of *Sleepless in Seattle* (1993) and *You've Got Mail* (1998), once said, "'There are two kinds of romantic leading men in American movies; there's the godlike person you never meet, like Cary Grant, and then there's the boy next door you've known all your life, like Jimmy Stewart." This precisely sums up the two types of leading men in a Hitchcock movie, and they are quite different from each other and used quite differently.

THE MAN HITCHCOCK WANTED TO BE — CARY GRANT

> *"One doesn't direct Cary Grant, one simply puts him in front of a camera."* — *Alfred Hitchcock*

Hitchcock once described Cary Grant as "The only actor I ever loved." He was someone that Hitch wanted to be — debonair, handsome, and popular with the ladies. Grant was cast as the American agent in *Notorious*, the suspect

Cary Grant, the man Hitchcock wanted to be, with Ingrid Bergman in *Notorious* (1946).

husband in *Suspicion*, the retired cat burglar in *To Catch a Thief*, and the slick advertising exec mistaken for a spy in *North by Northwest*. Hitchcock put himself in the leading man's role and wanted to woo beautiful, glamorous women such as Ingrid Bergman, Grace Kelly, and Eva Marie Saint. Through Cary Grant, he did that.

Today the numbers of real genuine men in Hollywood who can believably run away from a crop-duster in a crisp suit are rare. One possible contender for Grant's crown today is George Clooney. Think of his performance in *Intolerable Cruelty*, or in the *Ocean's Eleven* films. Other Cary Grant contenders include Hugh Grant in *Four Weddings and a Funeral* and *Notting Hill*, Hugh Jackman in *Kate & Leopold*, and Pierce Brosnan and Daniel Craig in the James Bond films.

THE MAN HITCHCOCK WAS — JAMES STEWART

Spying through windows, investigating a homicidal murder, falling in love with a duplicitous blonde, acting as a criminal investigator — these are all roles that could be described as belonging to both Alfred Hitchcock and James Stewart, his celluloid counterpart. Stewart played a professor in *Rope* who uncovers a murder committed by his former students, a photojournalist in *Rear Window* who passes the time by spying on his neighbors, a doctor on holiday whose son is kidnapped and who uncovers a plot to assassinate an ambassador in *The Man Who Knew Too Much*, and an emotionally crippled retired detective with a fear of heights in *Vertigo*. Stewart was an even bigger box office draw in some parts of America than Cary Grant, especially in the midwestern states where people identified with his folksy, boy-next-door charm and humility. He was the quintessential everyman of the time, a role he personified in such non-Hitchcock classics as

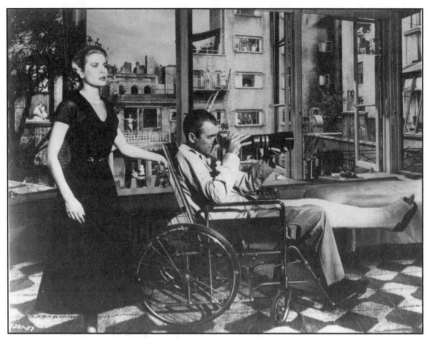

James Stewart, the man Hitchcock was, with Grace Kelly in *Rear Window* (1954).

Mr. Smith Goes To Washington (1939), *It's A Wonderful Life* (1946), and *Harvey* (1950).

Hitchcock often said that if he weren't a movie director, he would be a criminal lawyer. There's an amusing story of him and his film composer and good friend Bernard Herrmann doing the washing up one day after dinner. When Hitchcock was asked what he would be if not a director, he folded the tea towel and said very solemnly, "A hanging judge."

"I think Hitchcock was a man whose excitement in life was looking into someone else's life," says Robert Towne, screenwriter of *Chinatown* (1974). "You see it in Jimmy Stewart [in *Rear Window*], this All-American guy who was fascinated in the goings on in other people's bedrooms, much as Hitchcock is fascinated by these things, and his being confined to that room...until the outside world started looking at him. It's a cautionary tale and one of his most successful films in that way, and one of his most autobiographical."

When you think of leading men today who fit in James Stewart's shoes, Tom Hanks immediately comes to mind. Like Stewart, Hanks has captured the hearts of the American cinema-going public with his everyman appeal in films such as *Big*, *Sleepless in Seattle*, *Forrest Gump*, and *Saving Private Ryan*.

Elizabeth Perkins, Tom Hank's co-star in *Big*, also compares him to James Stewart. "I don't think anybody could have played that role in *Harvey* apart from Tom Hanks. Very similar actors when I think about it. You never see any affectation."

GLAMOROUS HEROINES

The quintessential Hitchcock heroine is cool, svelte, blonde, alluring, and mysterious. From the early days of Madeleine Carroll in *The 39 Steps* and *Secret Agent*, through to Ingrid Bergman in *Spellbound* and *Notorious*, and to Grace Kelly in *Rear Window* and *To Catch a Thief*, and Kim Novak in *Vertigo*, Hitchcock cast blondes who were impeccably dressed, mysterious and blonde. He tried again with Vera Miles in *The Wrong Man* and *Psycho*, Eva Marie Saint in *North by Northwest*, and lastly Tippi Hedren in *The Birds* and *Marnie*.

Hitchcock himself says that the casting of blonde heroines in his films was by accident and that his reason for casting actresses was to avoid the obvious sexy blonde. For Hitchcock it was important to distinguish between the big, bosomy blonde like Marilyn Monroe, and the ladylike blonde with the touch of elegance whose sex must be discovered. Grace Kelly was a rather mousy ingénue in Fred Zinnemann's *High Noon* (1952), but under Hitchcock's careful direction and supervision she blossomed into a sensual woman with an elegant veneer in *Dial M for Murder* and *Rear Window* (both 1954).

"I prefer a woman who does not display all of her sex at once — one whose attractions are not falling out in front of her," says Hitch. "I like women who are also ladies, who hold enough of themselves in reserve to keep a man intrigued. On the screen, for example, if an actress wants to convey a sexy quality, she ought to maintain a slightly mysterious air. When a man approaches her, the audience should be led to wonder whether she intends to shrink from him or tear off his clothes."

Hitchcock loved contrast, which is probably the reason he preferred ladylike women like Grace Kelly and Tippi Hedren. "As a movie director, I have found that an actress with the quality of elegance can easily go down the scale to portray less exalted roles. But an actress without elegance, however competent she may be, can hardly go up the scale to portray, let us say, an ambassador's wife. She lacks the range as an actress because she lacks the range as a person. A woman of elegance, on the other hand, will never cease to surprise you."

He often professed to his fondness for English women, the Scandinavians, the North Europeans, and the Germans, who behave like school marms, but when you get them in the back of a taxi, all sex would break loose. Grace Kelly, for example, epitomized the Hitchcock blonde, as her mother was German and her father Irish, while Tippi Hedren's ancestry was Swedish, Norwegian, and German.

Who are today's Hitchcock blondes? There's Jodie Foster in *Flightplan* (2005) and Naomi Watts in *Mulholland Dr.* (2001). Emily Blunt, Nicole Kidman, Cate Blanchett, Charlize Theron, Scarlett Johansson, and Michelle Williams have all also played Hitchcock-inspired heroines.

ATTRACTIVE VILLAINS

"The more successful the villain, the more successful the picture" — Alfred Hitchcock

Hitchcock has given us some of the most memorable villains ever to grace the screen. That's because he avoided the cliché through character and made his villains attractive.

"All villains are not black, and all heroes are not white. There are grays everywhere. You can't just walk down Fifth Avenue and say he's a villain and he's a hero. How do you know?" said Hitchcock. "In the old days, villains had moustaches and kicked the dog." But never in a Hitchcock film. "Very often you see the murderer in movies made to be a very unattractive man. I've always contended that it's a grave mistake, because how would he get near his victim unless he had some attraction?"

Uncle Charlie (Joseph Cotten) turns on the charm in *Shadow of a Doubt* (1943).

When you consider the roster of Hitchcock villains, such as Claude Rains in *Notorious*, Joseph Cotten in *Shadow of a Doubt*, Robert Walker in *Strangers on a Train*, Ray Milland in *Dial M for Murder*, James Mason in *North by Northwest*, Anthony Perkins in *Psycho*, and Barry Foster in *Frenzy*, they all have something in common; they are charming, sympathetic, and appealing. Hitchcock knew that evil was seductive and he was one of the first directors to cast handsome actors in murderous roles.

Claude Rains played a very touching villain in *Notorious* who is deceived by the woman he loves. "He is sympathetic because he is the victim of a confidence trick, and we always have sympathy for a man no matter how foolish he is," said Hitch, who also believed that the villain's love for the film's heroine was stronger than the hero's. We can't help but feel sorry for Alex (Rains) at the end, when he is summoned back into the house for questioning by his Nazi friends, to what is likely certain death. His love for Alicia (Ingrid Bergman) is sincere, and it's easier to sympathize with him than Cary Grant's cold "hero," Devlin.

In *Shadow of a Doubt*, Joseph Cotten also has the audience's sympathy, even though he is the "Merry Widow Murderer." In *Rope*, John Dall as Brandon, the instigator of the murder, is a much more attractive character than Farley Granger's rather insipid Phillip.

In both *Strangers on a Train* and *Psycho*, Hitchcock cast against type for the role of the psychotic killer. Robert Walker was well known for playing boy-next-door types and war heroes. So it was inspired casting when Hitchcock saw his potential and hired him as the disturbed, stalking psychopath Bruno Anthony in *Strangers on a Train*. Walker was more colorful than nominal hero Farley Granger, and even succeeded in making his villain more likeable than Granger's leading man. When Walker accidentally drops the incriminating cigarette lighter

John Dall's attractive psychopath overshadows Farley Granger's ineffectual co-conspirator in *Rope* (1948).

down a drain towards the climatic finale, the audience can't help but root for the film's villain to get it back and save himself. Such is the subversive ability of Hitchcock.

Anthony Perkins, like Robert Walker, was well-known for playing the All-American boy-next-door and attractive leading men. But Hitchcock saw the many facets of his character and his potential to play the disturbed Norman Bates in *Psycho*. In the source novel by Robert Bloch, Norman is fat and middle-aged and not sympathetic and you wouldn't switch your allegiance to him after Marion is killed in the shower. So Hitchcock and screenwriter Joseph Stefano changed him to being a sensitive young man. "I perceived a young man, vulnerable, good looking, kind of sad, makes you feel sorry for him," said Stefano, and it was Hitch who thought of casting Perkins. It turned out to be inspired casting, as Hilton Green, the AD on *Psycho* said, "Hitch was very impressed with Tony."

The role of the villain in the movie is sometimes split up between several characters. In *North by Northwest*, Hitchcock wanted to show a villain who was smooth and charming enough to attract a woman such as Eva Marie Saint's Eve into bed, so he cast the debonair actor James Mason to play central baddie Phillip Vandamm. Hitch never made him do a dastardly thing in the whole picture, he just had to nod to his henchmen.

Hitchcock also wanted a character that could look and act more threatening to Saint's well-being, so he created the character of Leonard (Martin Landau), a saturnine looking henchman. At the same time, he needed a heavyweight thug who would rough up Cary Grant's Thornill and who would kill the real Mr. Townsend at the United Nations by throwing a knife, so he cast veteran "bad guy" actor Adam Williams as Valerian.

Today's villains have taken a cue from Hitchcock and are charming, seductive, and attractive. Think of Alan Rickman in *Die Hard* (1988) or John Malkovich in *In The Line of Fire* (1993), or even Jonathan Rhys Meyers in *Match Point* (2005). They all exude charm and charisma and the audience will root for an attractive villain, sometimes wishing for them not to be caught by the police and literally get away with murder.

Sometimes the villain of the picture is not a person at all, such as in *The Birds*, where avian marauders attack the town of Bodega Bay. In *Jaws* (1975) the menace is a shark, in *The Fog* (1980) it's an unseen supernatural menace, and in *The Mist* (2007) it's mutant insects created through a military biological experiment.

SEX SCENES AND CENSORSHIP

"Sex on the screen should be suspenseful, I feel. If sex is too blatant or obvious, there's no suspense." — *Alfred Hitchcock*

Like all directors, Hitchcock knew that sex sells. He cast attractive actors and actresses and kept the sexual tension simmering with innuendo and risqué dialogue. It was also a clever way of getting around the censors with lines that were considered too daring at the time. In the dining car scene in *North by Northwest*, Eve says to Thornhill, "I never discuss love on an empty stomach," to which he replies, "But you've eaten," and she counter replies, "But you haven't." If you closely watch her lips moving, what Eva Marie Saint actually says is, "I never make love on an empty stomach." The line was too suggestive for the censors in 1959, so Hitchcock dubbed over it. But regardless, it's classic subtext.

Sex scenes in Hitchcock's films are suggestive rather than gratuitous. In today's liberal code anything goes, but in Hitchcock's golden era of the 1940s, '50s, and early '60s, the Hays Code, the movie's censorship guide, would not allow the depiction of the sexual act on celluloid. But Hitchcock overcame his battles with censorship, using suggestive dialogue and imagery. And it became a kind of game to see how far he could go with the censors.

In *To Catch a Thief*, Grace Kelly plays an American girl in the South of France, a rather frightening and aggressive example of the American debutante. In her first scenes Hitchcock deliberately filmed Kelly looking ice cold and kept cutting to her profile, looking classical, beautiful and distant. But for Hitchcock she wasn't frigid like the typical American woman, who is a tease — dresses for sex and doesn't give it. "That was epitomized by the kiss in the corridor. And the fireworks scene was a visual metaphor for sex," said Hitch.

North by Northwest is brimming with suggestive and sexy love scenes, but they are tastefully filmed. "In the love scenes, neither Cary Grant or myself took our clothes off and it was a very sexy scene," says Eva Marie Saint. Hitchcock couldn't at the time show the sexual act, and didn't want to, "Once you reach that point, where do you go?" he said.

His next film, *Psycho*, released a year after *North by Northwest*, starts off boldly. The camera catches a lingerie-clad Marion (Janet Leigh) and a shirtless Sam (John Gavin) in the aftermath of lunchtime sex in a seedy hotel. As Hitchcock explained, "I felt the need to do a scene of that kind because the audiences are changing. The straightforward kissing scene is looked down upon by the young people, and they would be inclined to say 'oh that's silly'...They themselves behave like Gavin and the girl, and you have to give them today the way they behave themselves most of the time." But as Hitchcock said, far be it for him as a Jesuit to encourage such a thing.

In *Topaz*, Hitchcock films Karin Dor's memorable death scene like a love scene between her and her lover, played by John Vernon. The camera circles the two bodies, and then the orgasmic jerk of her body as the bullet is fired into her, followed by a close-up of the gun. This scene aptly demonstrates what François Truffaut said of Hitchcock; "In America you respect him because he shoots scenes of love as if they were scenes of murder. We respect him because he shoots scenes of murder like scenes of love. Anyway, it's the same man we are talking about, the same man, and the same artist."

ACTORS AS CATTLE

"When an actor asks me what their motivation is, I reply 'Your salary!'" — *Alfred Hitchcock*

Hitchcock has often been accused of calling all actors and actresses "cattle." The quote was so infamous that during the shooting of *Mr. & Mrs. Smith* (1941), Carole Lombard, the film's star, brought three cows onto the set, each one labeled with the name of one of the film's stars.

This is what Hitchcock himself had to say about working with actors, "There is a dreadful story that I hate actors. Of course it may possibly be because I was once quoted as saying that actors are cattle. My actor friends know I would never be capable of such a thoughtless, rude and unfeeling remark, that I would never call them cattle... What I probably said was that actors should be *treated* like cattle."

No doubt that Hitchcock's remarks were intended as a joke, to shock and create publicity. Jim Brown, Hitchcock's AD on *The Birds* and *Marnie*, believed that remark was intended to add to Hitch's mystique and that "Deep down, I think he respected actors and actresses."

Despite his jocularity, many of Hitchcock's actors have remarked how sensitive and attentive he could be. He was able to coach his actors into giving him the performances that he needed to capture on screen. He didn't necessarily direct an actor, but discussed scenes with them in their dressing room or on the way to the set. As Hitchcock himself said, "I don't direct them, I talk to them, and explain to them what the scene is, what its purpose is, and why they are doing certain things, because they relate to the story and not to the scene."

"He was just Mr. Hitchcock, and a wonderful director," remembers Doris Day, who enjoyed working with Hitch on *The Man Who Knew Too Much*. Kim Novak agrees, "He was my favorite director, he was very precise, but he allowed you to find the emotion yourself, as long as you hit the marks. But he gave you so much freedom as an actor...he allowed me to do the emotions and be there."

Karin Dor says of her experience on *Topaz*, "Of all the directors I've worked with, Hitchcock was my favorite." Barbara Leigh-Hunt, who played the murdered Brenda Blaney in *Frenzy*, concurs. "He went out of his way to help me in the role. He was kindness personified, and if I queried something, he would always courteously explain it to me."

As Curtis Hanson, the director of *L.A. Confidential* (1997) and *8 Mile* (2002) says, "There's that ridiculous comment about actors being cattle, or whatever, that is attributed to Hitchcock. Be that as it may, the performances in *Rear Window*, from top to bottom, are brilliant, absolutely brilliant, as they were in many of Hitchcock's pictures."

BE HONEST WITH YOUR ACTORS

Although Hitchcock is widely known for his set pieces and bravado sequences such as the plane crash in *Foreign Correspondent*, the Albert Hall sequence in *The Man Who Knew Too Much*, and the shower murder in *Psycho*, there are some fine performances of light and shade in Hitchcock's films. Some memorable acting moments include Claude Rains in *Notorious*, as he confides in his mother in the middle of the night that he has unknowingly married an American agent, or Joan Fontaine shrinking from every appearance of Mrs. Danvers in *Rebecca*, Doris Day hearing the news that her son has just been kidnapped in *The Man Who Knew Too Much*, the obsessive efforts of James Stewart to reincarnate the image of Madeleine in Judy, both captivatingly played by Kim Novak, in *Vertigo*. The emotional power of all of these performances comes from both the artists involved and Hitchcock's direction.

Still, Hitchcock's reputation as not being an actor's director has stuck. Joan Fontaine (*Rebecca* and *Suspicion*) and Tippi Hedren (*The Birds* and *Marnie*) have both said that he could be controlling and manipulative. On *Rebecca*, Hitch intimidated the inexperienced Fontaine by telling her that co-star Laurence Olivier didn't want her in the part. Fontaine's subsequent portrayal as the young, nervous bride trying to please everyone is pitch perfect. Perhaps this was all part of Hitchcock's technique — creating in the actor the mood he wished the character to convey, in just the same way he directed Tippi Hedren in *Marnie* by keeping her in a state of isolation away from the other actors — perfect for the character, although perhaps not so much for the actress.

Despite being a self-confessed Svengali, Hitchcock himself said there was no fun in doing that all the time. Anthony Perkins loved working with Hitch and was encouraged to come up with his own ideas. It was Perkins' idea for his character Norman Bates to be eating candy corn while being interrogated by the detective Arbogast, played by Martin Balsam, and Hitch loved it. He said to both actors, "You both got a duologue here, why don't you go in a corner and have a go. You can't direct intelligent men, the things that should come to them naturally, such as hesitancies."

These scenes are just as masterful and emotionally effective as the set pieces that *Psycho* is known for. As Martin Scorsese says, "The acting is perfect. Balsam is friendly, but he slips in these probing, very embarrassing questions, just like a good private investigator, and as Perkins gets more uncomfortable he starts to stammer. The scene culminates with something so effective — simplicity itself. When Balsam points out the similarity between the handwriting sample and the signature in the book, he shows it to Perkins, who reluctantly cranes his neck down to look. Hitchcock brings the camera in for a tight close-up and moves with Perkins so that his head seems to turn in space, and his jaw line is accentuated, extended across the frame very animal like, just like one of his own stuffed animals. It's a reminder that Hitchcock began as a graphic artist, a talent he never really lost."

Hitchcock also elicited a wonderful performance from Robert Donat in *The 39 Steps* and once remarked to Norman Lloyd that Donat was his favorite leading man because he set the style for the wrongfully accused hero. "I could not have wished for a better Hannay than Robert Donat," said Hitch. "One of the chief reasons for his success — in addition, of course, to his natural looks, charm, and personality — is the good theatrical training he has behind him." Donat allowed other actors such as Cary Grant to add their interpretation of the wrongfully accused man. At the end of *To Catch a Thief*, when Grace Kelly says "Mother will love it here," Cary Grant improvised his character's comedic reaction.

Of her time working on *Vertigo*, Kim Novak remembers, "Oddly enough, Hitch gave me not much direction. Everything was about how the look was. He set up every scene physically to the mark, how you interpreted it, he left that to you. At first I was a little befuddled why there was so little direction, and I asked Jimmy Stewart about it, and he said that was just Hitch's way. But he was so very controlling of the exterior things."

Hitchcock gave direction to his actors only when they needed it. Eva Marie Saint remembers three specific directions during the filming of *North by Northwest*: "One, lower your voice. Two, don't use your hands. And three, look directly into Cary Grant's eyes at all times." Hitchcock wanted Eva to look more mysterious and with these instructions he gave her, "A sense of who this lady is. He was interested in shoes, hair, and in the exterior. I never felt he was telling me who the character was and he gave few directions. Hitch was very different to Elia Kazan who studied at the Lee Strasberg studio. During *On the Waterfront* Kazan would whisper things in my ear just before a take. He'd say the director is a conductor and should be able to play you like an instrument, but Hitch did not give that kind of direction." The result was a memorable performance by Eva playing a sexy double agent, quite different to her usual kitchen sink roles playing waifs. Tippi Hedren, who had no previous acting experience before starring in *The Birds* and *Marnie*, said that Hitchcock spent considerable time explaining her character's motivations and how he wanted a scene played.

Suzanne Pleshette, who worked with Hitchcock on *The Birds*, said, "As you talk to all the women who worked with Hitchcock, you will find, if they had experience, and if they could be trusted to use that experience to benefit the film, he in fact welcomed it. Those who were less experienced had to rely on his experience to take them through the various stages of the film."

When Karin Dor says goodbye to her character's lover in *Topaz*, she remembers "Hitchcock wanted to have me in tears when Juanita says goodbye. But I said, I would not cry when he is there, but when he left. He said OK, lets do it both ways. So we shot both versions and after he said 'you were right,' and he played my version in the finished film, which was very generous of him."

Jean Marsh agrees and enjoyed her collaboration with Hitchcock on *Frenzy*. There was a scene on which Jean and Hitchcock disagreed. Says Jean, "Hitch said 'OK, you can do it your way and I'll do it my way.' I've never known any other director doing that and it was so generous of him." On Hitchcock's tendency to be manipulative and Svengali-like when directing, Jean says, "That's a quick way of getting a response. You shouldn't have to do it if you are an experienced actress...Maybe he just did it with novice actresses, and not established ones."

Barbara Leigh-Hunt echoes Jean's sentiment about Hitchcock's collaborative nature. "He would say to me, 'Is your nose inside your face?' What he meant was could the camera see both my eyes for the take? Sometimes he would say 'Too many dogs feet' to an actor, and what he meant were 'pauses.' And during the scene when Barry Foster comes into the office and picks up the apple from my desk, the prop man asked Hitch where he should put the apple. Hitch asked me where my character would have placed the apple. So he gave me the courtesy to make a decision about where the apple should be."

Christopher Nolan, the director of *Insomnia* (2002), *Inception* (2010), and the *Batman* movies, has been described as the next Hitchcock. "We all grew up hearing about Hitchcock," he says. "What you find with actors, and I've really worked with some great actors, is that they are human lie detectors, and students of human behavior, and you cannot lie to them...Intelligent actors are very defensive, because they are often treated like idiots...so I find that I've had good relationships with actors through honesty."

Sensitive collaborator or cold Svengali, the fact remains that Hitchcock directed nine Oscar-nominated performances, and filled film after film with classic, unforgettable acting turns, something few directors can claim.

EXERCISES

1. Cite examples of how the casting has helped in Hitchcock's films *Notorious*, *The Wrong Man*, and *North by Northwest*. Why do the performances stand out? What makes the characters believable?

2. Think about the hero in your own movie. How would his character be different if he were played by Cary Grant compared to James Stewart? What attributes can you give your character to make him or her unique?

3. Write down a list of actors and actresses today who resemble Cary Grant, James Stewart, Ingrid Bergman, and Grace Kelly. What qualities do they have that resemble these stars? What roles do they tend to play?

4. Name some films where the main star is killed off earlier than expected. What effect does it have on the rest of the characters in the film? How do the audience's expectations change?

Key Hitchcock films to watch

Notorious (1945)
Strangers on a Train (1951)
North by Northwest (1959)
Psycho (1960)

Other directors' films to watch

Scream (1996)
The Dark Knight (2008)
Inception (2010)

Further reading

Directing Actors (1996) by Judith Weston
The Hitchcock Romance (1991) by Lesley Brill

CHAPTER FIVE

YOU HAVE A RECTANGLE TO FILL

"As the director, I have that rectangle to fill with a succession of images, one following the other. That's what makes a film."
— Alfred Hitchcock

itchcock was a master cinematographer, director, and technician, and perhaps understood the medium of film more than anyone. He knew how to hone his visual style so that the movie that he had created in his mind through careful planning, scripting, storyboarding, conferences and pre-production meetings looked like the one that is shot. He developed his own film language using unconventional camera angles, moving camera, and point of view to convey the feelings of his characters.

Along with a wonderful eye, Hitchcock knew instinctively where to put the camera, and it was always in the right place. "He used the phrase Camera Logic," says Norman Lloyd. "The camera is placed exactly where it should be to tell the story. When Janet Leigh is killed, the camera is exactly where it should be, the pull back from the eye. When I fall from the Statue of Liberty, that scene had to be worked without a cut. Hitch said we have to stay with me all the way to the bottom of the statue. That is storytelling, that is camera logic. This is what Hitch had to perfection." As Gil Taylor, his DP on *Frenzy* said, "Hitch was a 100% real director and the only one we've ever had...He never looked through my camera, not once. He would arrive on the set and give me a list of 12 shots for the day. Then, as soon as I said I was ready, he would bring all the actors to the set."

Some directors don't need to look through the camera, especially if they've worked with a DP or cinematographer who knows them well. Hitchcock famously boasted that he never needed to look through the camera lens. He was most interested in that rectangle to fill. When in doubt, draw a rectangle and then draw the shot for your cameraman.

USE A SUBJECTIVE CAMERA

Hitchcock was master of the subjective camera, and wanted to put the audience in the character's position to show how they felt. A subjective camera is used to match the emotional state of a character. Many of these camera techniques are industry standard, but Hitchcock used them better than just about anyone else. High- or low-angle shots indicate where the character is looking or feeling at a particular moment in time. A panoramic or panning shot is surveying the scene; a tracking shot or a hand-held camera shot signifies the character in motion. Subjective is opposite to objective, which is more like stage and theatre, where the audience is looking at the players on the stage. As production designer Robert Boyle said, "Hitchcock was most interested in feelings and was the most subjective director I know."

Often Hitchcock filmed a character from the front, and in close-up, so that the audience identifies with that character. The camera then precedes that character in each movement while keeping the character's size constant within the image. Then when he or she discovers something troubling, the camera will delay for a few seconds more on the face and look in order to heighten our curiosity. As Hitchcock said, subjective camera "is the way that you get a mental process going by use of the visual."

A good use of the subjective camera can be found in *Notorious* when Alicia (Ingrid Bergman) is introduced to all of Alex's (Claude Rains) Nazi friends and she has to convince them that she is a Nazi too and infiltrate herself into the group. By making the camera her eyes, Hitchcock conveys the intensity of the situation. As he said, "I wanted to say visually, here is Ingrid in the lions' den, now look at each lion!" Martin Scorsese praises the scene, "It's a subjective camera representing her viewpoint, but it has a very sneaky, unsettling effect, which is, of course, perfect, since she's been sent to Rio to spy on these people."

These insinuating camera movements are trademark Hitchcock. Very often when Hitchcock moves his camera, it's as if the camera were this invisible, sometimes ghost-like presence spying on the characters. This effect is most evidently felt in *Psycho*, a film built around voyeurism, from the opening track through the window to spy on Marion and Sam, to when Marion is packing to leave town, the camera picks up every detail. You see that she's packing to leave, and on her bed is the envelope with the money she's contemplating stealing. "It's pure, wordless exposition, and what makes it so disturbing is the feeling that there's another person in the room, making a ghostly inventory of every object, every move," says Martin Scorsese. This allows the audience to feel like they are involved in uncovering the story. Scenes can often begin by panning a room showing close-ups of objects that explain plot elements. This goes back to Hitchcock's beginnings in silent film. Without sound, filmmakers had to create ways to tell the story visually in a succession of images and ideas. Always use the camera as more than just a camera.

In *Vertigo*, Hitchcock uses subjective camera when Scottie kisses Judy in her Empire hotel room after he has remade her into the image of Madeleine. As Hitchcock said, "I had the whole set built in a circle, the stable, the last time he embraced her and the hotel room, and I made a plate of the whole thing, and I stood them on a little platform and turned them around. The whole thing was, instead of like they do in the movies, he dissolves and remembers the past, [in this way] he *felt* the past. I wanted to give the feeling that he felt it by doing that." For Hitchcock, putting the audience into Stewart's viewpoint was very important to show his state of mind, confusion, and then elation that Madeleine had returned from the dead.

John Carpenter, the director of *Halloween* (1978), agrees that Hitchcock reaches the pinnacle of subjective camera in the *Vertigo* kissing scene, "The definitive Hitchcock moment would have to be the '360 kiss' in *Vertigo*; James Stewart and Kim Novak, wrapped in each other's arms in that green hotel room, as the background gives way to the darkly haunted stables at the mission. Pure emotional cinema at its finest. The shot expresses Stewart's emotional state visually, which is, of course, the point of all Hitchcock movies."

The filming of *Rear Window* is purely subjective treatment; the camera sees what Jeffries (James Stewart) sees all the time across the open courtyard at the apartment buildings. The key opening scene in *Rear Window* sets up the voyeuristic theme of the film, as Hitchcock pushes the subjective camera to new heights. There will be more about this in the next chapter on editing and montage. Many of the camera techniques that Hitchcock used as part of his cinematic toolkit have become industry standard, but Hitchcock used them better than anyone else because of his use of the subjective treatment.

USE LENSES THAT MIMIC THE HUMAN EYE

Hitchcock's preferred lens was a 50mm because he said that was the lens of the human eye. A 50mm lens is often called a "normal" lens because objects remain in perspective approximately as they do with the human eye. As Hitchcock was so keen on subjective viewpoint and a character's point of view, he was very fond of using a 50mm lens, which is frequently used to give a character's point of view. The camera is the audience all the time, and they are seeing it with their own eyes.

In *Psycho* Hitchcock often used a 50mm lens to implicate the audience as fellow voyeurs. The camera becomes the people watching in the movie theater, as if they were spying on the characters, from the very first scene between Marion and Sam in the hotel room. In the scene where Norman is spying on Marion while she is undressing, this effect is most felt, and he implicates all of us as Peeping Toms. The scene also prepares the audience as our identification begins to shift from Marion to Norman.

When you look through the finder of a 50mm lens, which is about 2 inches, you see the perspective as the eye sees it. A 40mm lens has a wider angle and is good for two-shots. Now the moment you go to a 35mm lens, the perspective begins to change, to elongate, and more so with a 28mm lens. In other words, the wider the angle of lens, the more forced the perspective becomes. Hitchcock never liked to use wide-angle lenses, but preferred the 42mm or 40mm lens, which is slightly wider.

FRAME SHOTS FOR DRAMATIC PURPOSE

"The size of the image is very important to the emotion." — *Alfred Hitchcock*

Hitchcock was adamant that he would never film a shot without it having a clear dramatic purpose. That is a shot that moves the story and enhances the narrative. At the same time, he didn't shoot master scenes, but shot only what was necessary, unless it was a duologue. If you've got two people talking at a table, you shoot over-the shoulder shots and you have to repeat the scene, but otherwise not.

He also criticized Hollywood directors who would arrange and film a scene as if it were theatre. The actors move through the décor, they speak, and the camera films them in entirety in a master shot. Then the director shoots various closer shots, and then finally close-ups of the different actors. Each line of dialogue is then "covered" under a variety of angles. Later the editor will spend three or four months assembling the material while striving to give it rhythm, but without ultimately removing its theatrical side. This is the form of cinema recording that Hitchcock calls "photographs of people talking" and for Hitchcock this isn't utilizing film to its advantage.

Different angles have different subconscious effects. Hitchcock used framing size to plan out his scenes. These variations are a way of controlling when the audience feels intensity or relaxation. He compared his work to a composer writing a musical score — except instead of playing instruments, he's playing the audience. Hitch said it was like orchestration; it's not only the angle but also on the size of the image. Each set-up you use must contribute to the scene as a whole. Use the language of the camera and don't waste it. The audience shouldn't be aware of the size of image change.

Hitchcock framed his shots for emotion — for laughter, romance, anxiety, and loss. The first consideration of where to place the camera should involve knowing what emotion you want the audience to experience at the particular time. Emotion comes directly from the actor's eyes and you can control the intensity of that emotion by placing the camera close or far away from those eyes. A close-up will fill the screen with emotion, and pulling away to a wide angle shot will generally dilute that emotion.

When framing a shot, Hitchcock never thought about the geography of the set but always what would be on the screen. "Now, you see, when I'm on the set, I'm not on the set," he said, "If I'm looking at acting or looking at a scene — the way it's played, or where they are — I am looking at a screen, I am not confused by the set and the movement of the people across the set. In other words, I follow the geography of the screen. I can only think of the screen."

Alfred Hitchcock framing up for a shot.

For Hitchcock, keeping the shot wide is dull as it makes it so empty and so loose. Most directors say, "Well, he's got to come in that door so he's got to walk from there to there." Hitchcock felt the opposite. "Well, if he's still in a mood — whatever mood he's in," he said, "take him across in a close-up, but keep the mood on the screen." Hitch was not interested in distance, but the state of the mind of the character.

A sudden cut from wide to close-up will give the audience a sudden surprise. Sometimes a high angle above an actor will heighten the dramatic meaning. Hitchcock also was adamant that the size of the image on the screen must contribute to the story, for dramatic purposes rather than to establish background.

USE CLOSE-UPS TO INCREASE SUSPENSE

"If a character moves around and you want to retain the emotion on his face, the only way to do that is to travel the close-up." — *Alfred Hitchcock*

A close-up is a camera perspective in which the principal subject dominates the frame and is usually a close shot of a person or an object. There are two types of close-ups — extreme and medium. Hitchcock used close-ups frequently as he was always looking for more intimate ways to heighten suspense and tension. In the exciting climax to *Saboteur*, the hero factory worker Barry Kane (Robert Cummings) tries to save the villain Frank Fry (Norman Lloyd) from falling off the Statue of Liberty by holding onto his sleeve. Hitchcock, rather than keep the camera at a distance, cuts straight to Fry's coat and observes the painful rip of the shoulder seam, stitch by stitch. Hitchcock's characteristic remark was, "He should have had a better tailor!"

This scene has been replayed in subsequent films countless times. In *Die Hard* (1988), the sleeve is replaced by a watch, and in *Cliffhanger* (1993), by a glove. But Hitchcock later admitted that he made the mistake of not having the hero rather than the villain in danger from falling off the statue. This goes back to identifying with the hero as discussed in Chapter 4.

In a Hitchcock film, there is no air or redundant space around characters or above their heads. Close-ups are filmed for emotional impact. He often gave his cameramen specific instructions not to have any air around the figures. "He knows very well that when I compose I object to air, space around figures, or above their heads, because I think it's redundant," he said. "It's like taking a still like a newspaperman and trimming it down to its essentials. They have standing instructions from me."

"Hitch didn't like airspace, especially over the shoulders. He wanted the audience to concentrate on the actors," says AD Hilton Green.

Another reason for framing up close is because you may need space to use dramatically. In *The Birds*, when Melanie shrinks back on the sofa during the attack on the house, Hitchcock keeps the camera back to indicate the nothingness from which she was shrinking. Then he varies that sense of distance and space when he cuts back to her. He goes high, and then there is a movement up, and around. Had Hitchcock been close in the beginning, he would have shown Melanie shrinking from something possibly off screen. What Hitch wanted to show was that she was shrinking from nothingness, to convey her psychological fear. She doesn't know what she's shrinking from.

SAVE YOUR CLOSE-UPS FOR DRAMATIC EFFECT

An extreme close-up is, as the name implies, a tighter version of a close-up. Usually it's a shot of a small object or part of the face that fills the screen. For example, when the camera closes in on the face of a person and then comes in even closer to focus on an eye. Hitchcock's favorite expression for an extreme close-up was a "big head."

Hitchcock bemoaned the fact that sometimes in films you see close-ups that come in too early, so by the time you really need a close-up it has lost its effect because you've already used it. *Psycho* offers some great examples where the juxtaposition of image size is very important. As Hitchcock says, "One of the biggest effects in *Psycho* was where the detective enters the house and goes up the stairs. The shots were storyboarded to make sure there was enough contrast of sizes within the cuts...Here is the shot of the detective, a simple shot of going up the stairs, he reaches the top stairs, the next cut is the camera as high as it can go, it was on the ceiling. You see the figure run out, raised knife, it comes down, Bang! — The biggest head you can put on the screen...But the 'big head' [close-up] has no impact unless the previous shot has been so far away."

The long shot serves to accentuate the close-up. This is the size of the image put together to create shock. Hitchcock likens the choice of shot size to music — the brass sounding loud because you need it. If it were music it would be tremolos on the violins and suddenly a brass instrument, which is the big close-up, and from that Arbogast the detective falls. The moral of the story is don't go putting a close-up where you don't need it, because you may need that close-up later for dramatic effect.

USE MEDIUM SHOTS TO IDENTIFY WITH YOUR CHARACTER

A medium shot is a shot size intermediate between a long shot and a close-up. It's usually a shot of a person or several people from the waist up and typically they will occupy half to two thirds of the frame. The camera is sufficiently distanced from the character's body to be seen in relation to her or his surroundings. Mid-shots are very commonly used in indoor sequences to show the visual space between characters to help place them in context.

Hitchcock uses the medium shot to good effect in *The Man Who Knew Too Much* to make us identify with the character. In the film's climax at the Albert Hall, by showing Jo (Doris Day) in the medium shot, and always returning to her, Hitchcock makes us identify with her character. She is the helpless observer, unable to do anything but watch as the assassination attempt unfolds. In this way she suffers just as the audience watching the film does — worried, fearful for the life of the visiting Prime Minister.

The story is quickly explained without any dialogue through the editing and size of shots that Hitchcock chooses. As Jo enters the hall she looks for the assassin, who sits on the upper floor balcony, waiting for the orchestra to reach the key moment in the performance that will signal him to shoot the Prime Minister sitting across the hall. All the key characters are introduced in this sequence: Jo, the assassin, the Prime Minister, and the orchestra, and we are shown how they are all linked through Jo. By showing her in a medium shot, and always returning to her, Hitchcock makes us identify with her character. The above sequence also establishes the basic shot pattern that will be repeated throughout the rest of the sequence, which reminds the audience who is involved.

In Hitchcock's memos, Jo's shots are numbered and given a length for each shot: "Waist shot Jo hands by side. She turns to look left at Assassin's box (4 seconds); Waist shot Jo hands by sides looking at Assassin's box (4 seconds); Waist shot Jo still looking at Assassin's box, hands down. She closes her eyes crying and lowers head (6 seconds); MCS Jo crying still by curtains hands by sides. She puts right hand up to curtain, bag in right hand with gloves (10 seconds)."

Hitchcock makes slight changes to the shot sequence each time by varying or adding details that not only move the story along, but heighten the tension as well. For example, in one subsequent repetition of the sequence, Hitchcock takes us closer to each of the characters involved, which increases the impact of the emotions associated with each of them. When Hitchcock cuts to the assassin, it's a close-up, or a "big head," as the turning of his head to view the Prime Minister would be even slower and more noticeable at that proximity, making it more sinister. The sequence is key because it sets up the situation from the start, and allows Hitchcock to play with the audience's emotions from there.

DON'T USE LONG SHOTS JUST FOR ESTABLISHERS

A long shot is a camera shot taken from a long distance that shows landscape, other people, or a building, that usually includes a wide-angle field of view. In many films, the opening shot that establishes the environment is a long shot — it usually has a wide field of view and serves to orient the audience to the surroundings of the situation they are about to see.

Hitchcock thought that establishing shots were a waste of time but sometimes necessary. He was adamant not to just use his long shots for scene establishers and didn't shoot them indiscriminately, but he preferred to save the long shots for dramatic purpose when they were needed. "I never establish a room. That's why art direction in a film is so different from a stage. That is why I rely on the near objects in a room to give atmosphere," he said.

Take for example a man in the police station who comes in to turn himself in. Hitchcock will set the camera by the desk and the door but he doesn't reveal the whole set yet. His collaborators might ask, "Aren't you going to show it's a police station, the whole thing." But why? The sergeant has three stripes on his arm, near the camera, that's enough. That long shot may be very important to you in a dramatic moment — so why waste it.

Another effective use of the long shot for dramatic purposes occurs in *The Birds*, when Lydia Brenner (Jessica Tandy) goes to check on a neighbor at his farm. Lydia is driving her truck. Hitchcock is very careful to show the arrival of the truck along the long road — and had it watered down, because he didn't want dust to rise. He wanted instead for the dust to come up on the return, after Lydia has found the neighbor dead in his bedroom, his eyes pecked out by birds. That truck, seen at a distance at tremendous speed, expressed the frantic nature of her mood and in effect it becomes an emotional truck.

The long shot is also effectively used in *Marnie* when Marnie (Tippi Hedren) is robbing the Rutland safe. As Hitchcock said, "By presenting on the screen the girl at the safe and the danger of discovery, you show the two things at the same time — in a long shot. Not in the old-fashioned way they used to do in the movies, when you cut from one to another, that is not as potent to the audience as showing the two images together."

In *Torn Curtain*, when Michael (Paul Newman) crosses the farm, in the fields Hitchcock starts with a long shot. The moment he meets the farmer, he says, "Well, what does it feel like to be a dirty agent." Hitchcock bangs that both visually and aurally at the same time by going in close.

The best sequence in *Topaz* is a long shot and it occurs outside the Hotel Teresa in Harlem, between the French agent Dubois (Roscoe Lee Brown) and the Cuban secretary Uribe (Donald Randolph). Here Hitchcock has a genuine use of the long focus lens, as he describes it, "In real life if you stand across a very wide street, you are able to single out two individuals and watch them and exclude everyone else. But if you were to do that on film, the eye of the audience would never go where you wanted them to go. So there was a use of the long-focus lens singling out the two principles to the exclusion of all else." You still had a feeling that you were at a distance from them, because of all that was going on in front of the camera.

THE HIGH ANGLE

In a high angle shot, the camera looks down at what is being photographed. By shooting high you show a lot of space around a person, so there's a kind of loneliness and isolation around the figure. It's important not to use these shots indiscriminately. High angle shots are also used to create feelings of realization.

High angles are effectively used in *The 39 Steps*, *Shadow of a Doubt*, *The Wrong Man*, *North by Northwest*, *Psycho*, *The Birds*, and *Topaz*. They are often used to signify that a person is depressed or in a crisis. In *The 39 Steps*, after shooting "Mr. Memory," when Professor Jordan tries to escape, Hitchcock cuts to a high angle to increase the drama. When Uncle Charlie is being chased in *Shadow of a Doubt*, Hitchcock selects a high angle shot, as he put it, "For clarity of effect. It was like saying, here we are above a maze, where you can see both the exit and all the people who are trying to keep him from getting there."

Hitchcock also uses a high angle shot when a character comes to a pivotal realization, like the one young Charlie (Teresa Wright) experiences in *Shadow of a Doubt*. Charlie has gone to the local library looking for a missing newspaper story. She discovers an article confirming her worst nightmares and then she looks at the ring that her uncle has given her and discovers initials inside confirming that it belonged to one of his victims. Hitchcock cuts to a high, wide-angle shot of Charlie, exposing her vulnerability, as she suddenly realizes that her Uncle Charlie is the "Merry Widow Murderer." Hitchcock said, "I want the camera to go back, and like an intake of breath, she's saying 'Uhhhhh!'" That's what the camera did. It went right up and back and revealed her alone in the library. Hitchcock used the camera to articulate the character's feelings.

In *The Wrong Man*, Manny Balestrero (Henry Fonda) has just made the same spelling mistake as the robber, writing "cash draw" instead of "cash drawer," convincing the detectives that he is the same robber, so Hitchcock cuts to a high angle shot of Fonda. High angle shots are used effectively to show danger, as in *Vertigo* when Scottie is looking down the stairs in the bell tower, or when Thornhill runs from the United Nations building, and later on Mount Rushmore, in *North by Northwest*.

In *Psycho* Hitchcock cuts to a high angle shot when Mrs. Bates comes out of the bedroom to stab Arbogast, and later when she is being carried downstairs by Norman. Hitchcock deliberately used a high angle because he didn't want to cheat the audience by shooting from the back, which would suggest that he is deliberately concealing her face. This scene #69 was originally written to cut to a high angle when Norman goes up the stairs to fetch mother, but Hitchcock rewrote it so that the camera would stay at ground level shooting up as Norman goes up to his mother's room, and starts moving after he gets into an off-screen argument with her. During all this, as Hitchcock said, "The camera has been creeping up the stairs. It does not stop at the top, however, but continues on the same high angle as in scene #57 when Arbogast was stabbed."

The scene was filmed as written, using the same set-up devised for the shot that descends to the key in *Notorious*, namely a cage hung from rails on the ceiling. This shot was very complicated and was rehearsed for a week as the grips worked with the camera operator on the timing and movement of the camera. In most of his movies, Hitchcock always had one or two shots that made the audience wonder how he achieved it, and in *Psycho* this was all done in one shot.

In *The Birds*, Hitchcock wanted a high angle shot of the birds attacking the town of Bodega Bay. "I did that high shot for three reasons," he said. "The first was intended to show the beginning of the gulls' descent on the town. The second was to show the exact topography of Bodega Bay, with the town, the sea, the coast, and the gas station on fire, in one single image. The third reason is that I didn't want to waste a lot of footage on showing the elaborate operation of the firemen extinguishing the fire. You can do a lot of things very quickly by getting away from something."

The most memorable shot in *Topaz* is a high angle shot of Juanita's death. Karin Dor vividly remembers Hitchcock describing and planning the scene. "He said I want to see you falling in a pool of blood," Karin remembers, referring to the purple dress her character wears that splays open like blood. The dress was a kind of jersey, and they rehearsed for hours using a stand-in. Eight wires were attached to the seam of the dress, and at every end there was a technician who pulled the wires and the dress splayed out. The result was a truly memorable and poetic death, filmed from above. "Death cannot change beauty, it goes on," said Hitchcock in an interview.

THE LOW ANGLE

In a low angle shot, the camera looks up at what is being photographed. Generally it's used to show a character looking dominant, as in the case of the rape scene in *Marnie*. Hitchcock uses a low angle shot of Mark (Sean Connery) to convey his dominance over Marnie (Tippi Hedren) in a key scene. There are many low angle shots in *Psycho* of the Bates house to show it looming and sinister, the vertical motif being in opposition to the horizontal plane of the motel. When Norman is talking to Marion in the parlor, Hitchcock cuts to a low angle shot of Norman with a stuffed owl behind him, to show that he too is like a bird of prey. The low angle, together with Anthony Perkins' angular features and the harsh lighting, makes him look frightening and sinister.

The low angle is also used to get a variation or an abnormality. When Ben (James Stewart) discovers that his son has been kidnapped in *The Man Who Knew Too Much*, Hitchcock cuts to a low angle shot of Stewart as he nervously thumbs the phone directory in anxious trepidation.

USE CAMERA MOVEMENT TO KEEP THE MOOD

Hitchcock believed in moving the camera when it helped tell the story. "One of the first essentials of the moving camera is that the eye should not be aware of it, but should be on the character moving," said Hitch. "Imagine you have a scene between two people in a quarrel, a man and a woman. And you've got them on a sofa in a close shot, cutting just below head and shoulders, the two of them, and the girl gets up angrily and walks across the room. I will follow her in close-up across the room to maintain the mood. But very often this isn't done; a cut back to a long shot is used instead. Because the mood of the woman's emotional disturbance is there, you should never cut back — at least not until she gets over it and calms down. Then you can ease the camera out, ease it back unobtrusively."

Some camera movements used in Hitchcock's films include:

Pan — the camera moves horizontally on a fixed base.

Tilt — the camera points up or down from a fixed base.

Crane — the camera moves up or down through space.

Tracking or Dolly Shot — the camera moves through space on a dolly but stays in the same plane.

TRACKING SHOTS

" The eye must look at the characters, it must not be conscious of the camera dollying, unless you are dollying in for the purpose, then you should make the audience conscious of a zooming in or cutting. " — Alfred Hitchcock

Rebecca was the first film in which Hitchcock experimented with a tracking camera, because he wanted to move around the big house of Manderley and imply the ghostly presence of the first Mrs. de Winter. In the famous opening of *Shadow of a Doubt*, the theme of the double is established by Hitchcock's tracking camera — as it introduces Uncle Charlie and Niece Charlie in parallel viewpoints; six shots consistently right for Uncle Charlie and six shots consistently left for Niece Charlie. The successive shots show the larger view of the respective cities, the exteriors of the houses, then the windows, then a slow dolly to each Charlie lying fully clothed on a bed.

Hitchcock also used the tracking camera to create emotional mood. One of the most famous tracking shots occurs in *Notorious* during the balcony kiss between Devlin and

Alicia (Cary Grant and Ingrid Bergman). "I didn't want to cut there because I wanted to retain an embrace," he said. "I felt that the camera, we should all embrace, they should remain in their embrace and we should join them. And [so I] followed them, never left the close-ups, all the way to the telephone and up to the door, a continuous shot. The whole idea was about not breaking the romantic notion. So it was an emotional thing, the movement of that camera."

The intention is to keep the audience with the embrace, so that when Grant and Bergman go to the phone, the camera follows them, never leaving the close-up all the way, right up to the phone and over to the door, all in a continuous shot. Hitchcock didn't want to cut up the sequence so he used the movement of the camera to maintain the emotional intensity. This two and a half minute kissing scene in *Notorious* is famous for being an attempt to get around the censors, as at the time on-screen kisses could only last three seconds, so Hitchcock cleverly got around this by simply having the actors break apart every three seconds before they resumed kissing. Sometimes dollying is done in more subtle ways in keeping with the mood. In *Torn Curtain*, when Michael (Paul Newman) says to the professor "My God, it's brilliant" as he realizes the secret formula, so Hitchcock dollies in subtly.

In 1991's *Cape Fear*, Martin Scorsese uses traditional subjective camera as he travels down the corridor when Danielle (Juliette Lewis) goes to meet Max (Robert De Niro) in the school auditorium. Danielle goes down the aisle to the stage. But it becomes a scene that's inspired by the undercurrents in the Hitchcock pictures, where both Danielle and Max are in medium shots. But the camera doesn't move in those cases, and that has to do with, certainly, the quieter scenes in Hitchcock. There's so much more than just quick cutting and shock moments.

A subjective camera is used in one of Hitchcock's favorite techniques — the forward tracking shot to convey a character's point of view. This is effectively used in *Psycho* when Lila (Vera Miles) approaches the Bates house. The audience identifies with Lila and is just as curious to find out what is inside. Hitchcock uses a forward tracking shot in *Topaz* when Juanita (Karin Dor) is ordered to come down by Rico (John Vernon), who has just discovered that she is a traitor to her country. The subjective tracking shot puts the audience in the position of the character. "The point is to draw the audience right inside the situation instead of leaving them to watch it from outside, from a distance. And you can do this only by breaking the action into details and cutting from one to the other; so that each detail is forced in turn on the attention of the audience and reveals its psychological meaning," said Hitchcock.

Many directors have been influenced by Hitchcock's subjective camera. John Carpenter uses the subjective camera for when Laurie (Jamie Lee Curtis) is approaching the Wallace house in *Halloween* (1978) in just the same way as Hitchcock used for Lila (Vera Miles) in *Psycho* as she climbs up the steps to investigate the Bates house. David Fincher also cites Hitchcock as an influence, "I was a big Alfred Hitchcock fan...I've probably seen *Rear Window* sixty times. I know his movies inside and out." There are many Hitchcock pans and tracking shots and styling in Fincher's movies.

THE "*VERTIGO* SHOT"

Probably the most famous shot in *Vertigo* is a camera technique that causes the image to "stretch" — creating the illusion of the shot's background suddenly moving farther away from the camera. It has become known by many nicknames, including the *Vertigo* Shot, the Dolly Zoom, the Zolly, and even the Hitchcock Zoom. It took

Hitch twenty years to get the effect he wanted, and it's truly memorable.

In *Vertigo* the main character, Scottie Ferguson (James Stewart), suffers from agoraphobia and a fear of heights. Hitchcock wanted to convey Scottie's tremendous fear through cinematic techniques, so he devised the dolly zoom. The idea first came to Hitchcock years earlier when he was at the Chelsea Arts Ball in London. He had drunk too much, and at 2 a.m. everything around him seemed to be getting farther and farther away. Later, when he moved to America, he remembered the effect and wanted to use it in *Rebecca*. There's a scene in the movie when Joan Fontaine's character is supposed to faint at a coroner's inquest, and Hitchcock wanted the effect of everything going away from her, but he wasn't able to pull it off. He tried every technique, even printing a photograph on rubber and stretching the middle.

Later, when he was making *Vertigo* and trying to visually interpret Scottie's condition, he remembered that effect. He finally achieved it with a combination of a zoom lens and a dolly back, with the camera zooming in and the camera dollying back simultaneously, causing a visual perspective distortion, the most directly noticeable feature being that the background appears to change size relative to the central subject.

When Hitchcock asked the technical department how much the required overhead set-up would cost, they said it would be $50,000 because they'd have to take a rig above the staircase to take the camera up as the lens zoomed forward. "So I said yes, but there's no one on the set. Why don't we make a miniature of it, then lay it on its side, and do the same thing from the studio floor?" said Hitchcock. "The effect cost $19,000."

Zoom shots use a variable focal length lens to bring the audience closer or farther away from the scene. With the *Vertigo* Shot, Hitchcock creates a tremendous feeling of disorientation, which is what the character is feeling at that moment, by moving the camera back, then zooming forward, so magnifying the impression of depth. Again, just like the tracking shot, Hitchcock was using his camera technique to convey to the audience the character's emotional state.

The famous shot in *Vertigo* (1958), a dolly and zoom combined to give the "vertigo" effect.

Dolly zooms and zooms in general were popular in the '70s, but because they are unnatural for the human eye, and are therefore often a bit disconcerting to the audience, they are rarely used in today's films. Now cinematographers use the zoom very sparingly and prefer to move the camera instead.

The *Vertigo* Shot has become justifiably famous and has been imitated many times by other directors. In *Jaws* (1975), Steven Spielberg uses it when Chief Brody (Roy Scheider) first becomes aware that there is a shark near the beach full of swimmers. Spielberg dollies into Brody's face, while the beach background appears to recede. A relatively slow and more subtle *Vertigo* Shot can also be seen in Martin Scorsese's *Goodfellas* (1990). During a conversation scene between Henry and James (Ray Liotta and Robert De Niro) in a diner, Scorsese gradually dollies back and zooms in, causing the view outside the diner windows to distort while the subjects (Henry and James) remain unchanged.

Sam Raimi's western *The Quick and the Dead* (1995) uses the camera to dramatize the gunfights in the most visually exciting and melodramatic way possible. In one fight, Raimi wanted to see if he could use the *Vertigo* technique from Hitchcock -- zooming in and dollying back at the same time — to build suspense leading up to the moment of gunfire.

THE CRANE SHOT

A crane shot is where the camera is mounted on a crane, allowing it to move very high and then swoop back down to the ground. Sometimes the crane is mounted on a dolly, and the camera can move along the ground, while at the same time move up into the air. Hitchcock has majestic crane shots in *Young and Innocent, Notorious, Psycho, Marnie*, and *Topaz*, as he liked to have scenes that made the audience wonder how they were achieved.

In Hitchcock's *Young and Innocent* (1937) there's a magnificent crane shot that took two days to shoot. Set in a ballroom, the camera swoops across the dance floor while the characters search for the murderer, before finally settling on a drummer disguised in the band, who is revealed to be the killer by his nervous eye twitch in big close-up. Another very famous and even more elaborate crane shot occurs in *Notorious* which starts from high above during a party, down a staircase and keeps moving in on Alicia (Ingrid Bergman) at the bottom, going right into her hand, which is holding a key. "That's using the visual, that's a statement," says Hitchcock. "In this crowded atmosphere there is a very vital item, the crux of everything. So taking that sentence as it is, in this crowded atmosphere, you go to the widest expression of that phrase, so you go down to that vital thing, a little tiny key in the hand. That's the visual expression to say that everyone is having a good time, but you don't realize it, and there is big drama going on here and that big drama is epitomized itself in that tiny key."

The crane shot in *Notorious* is an example where the sweeping movement of the camera registers emotion and a long shot becomes an extreme close-up. To achieve this shot, Hitchcock used a hanging camera, with the camera suspended from a rail on the ceiling of the studio, and it was enhanced when it was being printed by an optical move in to an extreme close-up of the hand.

The crane shot is also used to great effect for a party scene in *Marnie*. Hitchcock wanted the same feeling of starting wide and then coming in and ending on a close shot of a character — in this case Strutt, Marnie's previous employer, whom she robbed. The actual movement of the camera creates suspense in the audience, as Hitchcock says, "Because you know it's going somewhere. So, it's like, 'Where is he going? Where is he going? Where is he going?' And it ends up on a close-up of Strutt, and

The famous crane shot in *Notorious* (1946), which was a mounted camera hanging from a rig suspended on rails from the ceiling.

the audience saying, 'Oh, my God!' This fellow who has just walked in through the door could unmask Marnie. It's visual storytelling and is involving the audience, kind of unconsciously."

To achieve the crane shot in the party scene of *Marnie*, a spectacular case of grip technique was needed. A team of grips was under DP Robert Burks' direction in order to unload pieces of the camera and dolly, set up the photography equipment, and move the camera and dolly during shots; the chief member of this team is called the "key grip" and his principal responsibility was for camera movement. Burks shot from a vantage point on the balcony overlooking the set of the spacious foyer of the Rutland estate house. As the doorbell sounds and a butler opens the door to various guests, the camera moves, in one fluid crane shot with modulated focus, twenty feet down to floor level and forty feet forward to swoop into the face of the entering guest, Strutt.

Another case of prestigious grip occurs in the killing of the detective Arbogast, played by Martin Balsam, in *Psycho*. Hitchcock wanted a special shot following Balsam down the stairs after having been stabbed at the top by Mrs. Bates. Hitch wanted to follow him all the way down to the bottom, just as he had done in *Saboteur* with the villain falling off the Statue of Liberty. Hitchcock and his crew made a rig with a chair that Balsam sat back on, and they were able to turn it. Balsam just sat there looking straight up, and he flailed his arms around as if falling back. Then Hitchcock shot a process plate down the staircase off this other rig and put the two pieces of film together to create the effect of Balsam falling down the stairs. As Hitchcock described the scene, "When a person falls, they are fighting the fall, they don't just drop back. If you are falling back, there is an effort to prevent it, and you get that effect there. It was double printed. He didn't fall back a single stair, and he sat in a very comfortable chair and lay there like that."

Director William Friedkin, who used the same technique in *The Exorcist* (1973), says, "Well, frankly, [in *The Exorcist*] it's a shot of a character being grabbed by the scrotum by the young girl who was possessed, and he falls backward, screaming. And I attached the camera to him. I found out how Hitchcock did that effect. He attached the camera to [the actor]...and that's what we did."

USE LONG TAKES FOR EMOTIONAL INTENSITY

A long take occurs when a long sequence of film is made without stopping the camera. Hitchcock said that he was willing to work with the long uninterrupted shot, but if he had to shoot continuously, he felt he was losing his grip on it, from a cinematic point of view. The camera is simply standing there, hoping to catch something with a visual point to it. What he liked to do was to photograph just the little bits of a scene that he really needs for building up a visual sequence in montage, which we will be discussing in Chapter 6.

But long takes can be used to evoke a huge array of emotions, and Hitchcock employs it to maximum effect in two of his films, *Rope* (1948) and *Under Capricorn* (1949). In *Rope*, Hitchcock filmed each scene in segments lasting up to ten minutes (the length of a reel of film at that time). Some transitions between reels were hidden by having a dark object fill the entire screen for a moment, such as a person walking into or past the camera. Hitchcock used those points to hide the cut, and began the next take with the camera in the same place.

As Hitchcock said of his long take experiment in *Rope*, "I got the crazy idea of seeing if I could do it all in one shot, the whole film...when I look back it's quite nonsensical because I was breaking my own tradition of using the cutting of film to tell a story. On the other hand, I approached it as if it was precut, so the camera movement and the movement of the players joined these cuts together."

Hitchcock approached *Rope* as if it were pre-cut with the movement of the players, but still kept to the size of the image and the relation in important moments. In the unity of the camera and photography, there's also a flow of light change as the sun sets outside the apartment windows. "The film played in its own time, there were no dissolves, no time lapses, there was only continuous action and I felt I ought to have a continuous flow of camera narrative with it," said Hitch.

Despite the great trouble Hitchcock went to in order to achieve these long takes, they do have their advantage for weight, conviction, and presence, a specific gravity that a heavily edited sequence might lack. Long takes keep the audience rooted in the story, not just as a passive observer, but also as a participant in the drama, drawing them into the unfolding of the drama. In *Under Capricorn*, Ingrid Bergman has a nine-minute confession scene all in one take, where the audience hears the truth about her character Henrietta's past at the same time as her confessor and friend, Charles Adair, played by Michael Wilding. The long take in the confession scene allows us to share Adair's reactions as he feels them in real time — shock and, ultimately, compassion, as Henrietta's story unfolds — as well as the cathartic effect it has on Henrietta.

Other non-Hitchcock examples of extended long shots include Orson Welles' opening shot of *Touch of Evil* (1958). This shot was a large step up from Hitchcock's experiment because of the extensive movement of the camera. The camera travels all over a small, bustling U.S./Mexico bordertown, starting on a bomb being placed in the trunk of a car and then following a couple (played by Charlton Heston and Janet Leigh) crossing through a border checkpoint. The sheer length of the take heightens the tension for the payoff at the end — the bomb exploding.

In *Goodfellas* (1990) director Martin Scorsese uses the long take to similar effect. The camera tracks the movements of a couple (Ray Liotta and Lorraine Bracco) on a date as they go from a car, across a street, through a nightclub's side door, down a flight of stairs, through a kitchen, and finally into the nightclub and to their reserved table. "The whole idea was that it had to be done in one take," says Scorsese. "The camera flowed through them and glided through this world, just all the doors open to him. Everything slipped away. It was like heaven." Like Hitchcock, Scorsese used the camera to convey the feelings of the central characters.

Another famous opening long take occurs in Robert Altman's *The Player* (1992). The shot takes place entirely outside on the grounds of a Hollywood studio. The camera tracks and picks up pieces of conversation from several characters, all setting up and providing the backstory for the film. Altman innovatively overlaps the conversations as he moves from one to the next. Other famous long takes can be seen in *Hard Boiled* (1992), *Boogie Nights* (1997), *Magnolia* (1999), and *Children of Men* (2006).

POINT OF VIEW

The subjective camera is linked to the reaction shot and point of view. The reaction shot is any close-up that illustrates an event by showing instantly the reaction to it of a person or group and gives the camera emphasis. The door opens for some one to come in, and before showing who it is you cut to the expressions of the persons already in the room. Or, while one person is talking, you keep your camera on someone else who is listening.

Putting an idea into the mind of the character, without explaining it in dialogue, is done by using a point of view. You take the eyes of the characters and add something for them to look at. In *Spellbound* (1945) two unprecedented point-of-view shots were achieved by constructing a large wooden hand (which would appear to belong to the character whose point of view the camera took) and out-sized props for it to hold: a bucket-sized glass of milk and a large wooden gun. For added novelty and impact, the climactic gunshot was hand-colored red on some copies of the black-and-white print of the film.

In *The Birds* there's a subjective point of view from Melanie after the sparrow attack down the chimney. Melanie represents the audience here — to show them that the mother (Jessica Tandy) is getting a bit unbalanced, and represents the general way Hitchcock handles a subjective point of view. He shows reverse cuts of Melanie's point of view and thus her increasing concern for the mother. Even when she crosses to Mitch, Hitchcock takes her across the room in the biggest close-up because he's walking with her. That's because her concern and her interest must be in the same size in the screen.

Sometimes the subjective point of view may shift between characters. For instance, at the end of *North by Northwest*, we shift our identification from Thornhill, who is entering Vandamms' house, to Vandamm's henchman Leonard, who suddenly realizes that Eve is a spy, and finally to Eve herself. This sets up the tension admirably between the characters for a very exciting climax.

As director Eli Roth says, "Hitchcock was really one of the first directors who understood how to use that subjective camera point of view of watching what was happening to create suspense. I love that. I mean, I will definitely do that. Even before Josh is killed in *Hostel*, the whole opening shot where we don't know where we are or what this place is, it's all shot through a little hole in a bag and it's just sort of looking around the room. And we're just getting little pieces of information as the character gets it. I mean, you can trace that going all the way back to *Rear Window*."

LIGHT YOUR FILM STYLISTICALLY

Lighting can play an integral role in enhancing a movie's overall look. Hitchcock believed that cameramen, who normally rose up the ranks in the studio starting as assistants, should be sent into the art galleries and study the Dutch masters like Vermeer to gain an understanding on the logic of light.

Hitchcock's best movies are like dreams and nightmares the way they are lit and filmed. As Hitch says, "When you have a nightmare, it's awfully vivid if you're dreaming that you're being led to the electric chair. Then you're as happy as can be when you wake up because you're relieved. It was so vivid. And that's really the basis of this attempt at realistic photography, to make it look as real as possible, because the effects themselves are actually quite bizarre. The audience responds in proportion to how realistic you make it. One of the dramatic reasons for this type of photography is to get it looking so natural that the audience gets involved and believes, for the time being, what's going on up there on the screen."

Lighting in the movies is something usually used to establish mood. Hitchcock used it to establish character. The lighting in *Strangers on a Train* symbolically indicates the true nature of the characters as dark and light. During the opening scene, where Bruno and Guy are talking in the dining car, Bruno sits so that the shadow of the compartment's blinds hits his face directly. The shadows are horizontal and resemble the bars of a jail cell. In contrast, no shadows darken Guy's face. Even before ten minutes of the film have passed, the lighting sends a subliminal message that Bruno's character is shady and not meant to be trusted. Hitchcock used this same effect all the way back in *The Lodger* (1927). When the killer goes to a window, Hitch makes the shadow of the window's lattice fall across the character's face in a way that suggests fractured menace.

Later in *Strangers on a Train*, once Bruno has killed Guy's wife Miriam, another display of symbolic lighting occurs. Bruno stands behind a gate across the street from Guy's house, far enough into the shadows so that his face is not visible. He calls Guy over to tell him the news, and Guy leaves the entrance of his brightly lit house to speak with Bruno. Guy stands in the light while they speak but once the police arrive at his house to inform him of the murder, Guy also hides in the shadows with Bruno behind the gate. This move into the shadows symbolizes Guy's complicity in the crime. But once Guy decides he wants nothing to do with Bruno, he storms out of the shadows and back to his house, as he decides to oppose Bruno for the remainder of the movie.

In *Vertigo*, Hitchcock reaches the pinnacle of film lighting and he and his cinematographer Robert Burks used an array of diffusion filters of various densities, including fog filters and green filters, used singly and in various combinations. When Hitchcock wanted Madeleine to look mysterious in the churchyard at Mission Dolores, which is the oldest building in San Francisco, he shot it through fog filters to create the illusion effect through sunshine. This scene in *Vertigo* was the first to be filmed, and it took the crew a day and a half to achieve the exact lighting effects that Hitchcock wanted.

As Hitchcock said, "You see, in the earlier part — which is purely in the mind of Stewart, when he is watching this girl go from place to place, when she is really faking, behaving like a woman of the past — in order to get this slightly subtle quality of a dreamlike nature, although it was bright sunshine, I shot the film through a fog filter and I got a green effect, fog over bright sunshine. If you're doing this in black and white pictures, and you're doing a fog scene, you can put a filter over the camera that is called a fog filter. I put fog over a scene of bright sunshine and it had another effect."

Later when Scottie follows Judy to her hotel, Hitchcock deliberately chose the Empire Hotel on Post Street because it had a green light outside. He used the same fog filter as in the churchyard. "That's why, when she comes out of the bathroom, I played her in the green light," says Hitch. "I wanted to establish that green light flashing all the time so that when we need it, we've got it. I slid the soft fog lens over, and as she came forward, for a moment he got the image of the past. Then as her face came up to him, I slipped the soft effect away, and he came back to reality. She had come back from the dead, and he felt it, and knew it, and probably was even bewildered — until he saw the locket — and then he knew he had been tricked." As Hitchcock says, there was a lot of interesting camera trickery in *Vertigo*.

EXERCISES

1. Watch the scene in *Psycho* where Arbogast climbs up the stairs and note where Hitchcock inserts close-ups, medium shots, and long shots. How do they contribute to the suspense of the story?

2. What emotions do we experience alongside the characters in *Psycho* during the following POV shots: Marion's driving sequence; Norman and Marion talking in the parlor; Norman spying on Marion; Lila walking up to and exploring the Bates house. How does it contribute to our feelings for the character?

3. What sensations are caused by the "stretching" Dolly Zooms in *Vertigo* and the opening shot of *Rear Window*? How do they express the feelings of the characters?

4. How do the crane shots in *Notorious* and *Marnie* contribute to the key moments of the plot?

Hitchcock films to watch

Strangers on a Train (1951)
Rear Window (1954)
Vertigo (1958)
Psycho (1960)
The Birds (1963)
Marnie (1964)

Other directors' films to watch

Cape Fear (1991)
Caché (2005)
Shutter Island (2010)

Further reading

Hitchcock at Work (2000) by Bill Krohn
Film Directing Shot by Shot (1991) by Steven D. Katz

CHAPTER SIX

THE ART OF CUTTING

"Art is emotion, therefore the use of film, putting it together and making it have an effect on the audience, is the main function of filming. " — Alfred Hitchcock

"Perfect cutting." That's the old-fashioned term Hitchcock used to describe the editing of his movies. Editing is the foundation of film-making, and no one knew this better than Hitchcock, who used images, not words, to communicate ideas and create emotion. He cut between parallel actions to build suspense; he created shock by cutting from one image size or angle to another; and he cut between character points of view to give sudden changes of perspective. It was in the editing suite that his films came alive. Hitchcock's use of editing, just like his cinematography, was to create an emotional response in the audience.

CUT THE FILM IN YOUR HEAD

"I don't shoot all kinds of angles. That would be like a musician trying various kinds of notes for one particular note. Well that's ridiculous. For me there's only one note needed, and that note is the right one. And so it is with the cut." — **Alfred Hitchcock**

When Hitchcock first came to America to direct *Rebecca* in 1939, he was under contract to David O. Selznick, the legendary producer. Selznick was accustomed to having his own way in post-production, but he soon discovered that Hitchcock had everything preplanned and tended to edit in his head; i.e., he only shot what he thought he needed. Today directors strive to attain this "final cut," which is the contractual ability to decide the final cut of the movie before its release. Hitchcock guaranteed himself final cut by only shooting the cut he had pre-planned.

Selznick complained about what he called this "jigsaw cutting" of Hitchcock's rather than the common Hollywood practice of ordering shots filmed from several angles and then choosing the best one during the edit, which gives much more flexibility. In fact at the end of editing *Rear Window*, there's a famous story that George Tomasini, Hitchcock's editor, took all the trims and outtakes and put them all on one reel. That shows just how little footage there was that wasn't used because Hitchcock knew exactly what he wanted and filmed only what he intended to edit. With most directors, a lot of film is left on the cutting room floor, but Hitchcock knew exactly what shots he wanted and didn't want to waste time on film he wasn't going to use.

Some directors like to edit their own movies, but Hitchcock never found it necessary to do more than supervise the editing of a film himself. During the making of *Psycho*, script supervisor Marshall Schlom recalls that Hitchcock would come into the editing suite at 11 a.m.

**Martin Balsam and Anthony
Perkins in *Psycho* (1960).**

and sit with editor George Tomasini for a few hours. For eight weeks while the film was being edited, he would assemble sequences in a "stop and go room" where the film was projected onto a big screen.

Hitch believed that if a scenario was planned out in detail, and followed closely during production, then editing the film would naturally follow. All that needed to be done was edit out any unnecessary details or sequences that did not advance the story, and then the finished film should be an accurate rendering of what was initially planned.

MONTAGE

> *"Oh, well a cut is nothing. One cut of film is like a piece of mosaic. To me, pure film, pure cinema, is pieces of film assembled. Any individual piece is nothing. But a combination of them creates an idea."* — *Alfred Hitchcock*

Montage is the process of editing where one shot, a strip of film or take, is joined with another; the shots can picture events and objects in different places at different times. Hitchcock often referred to the use of montage and the effect of what he called "pure cinema" to create an emotional response in the audience, namely "the complementary pieces of film put together, like notes of music make a melody." The point is that pure film is montage, which is the assembly of pieces of film, which in their turn must create an emotion in the audience. That is the whole art of the cinema — the montage of the pieces.

Among the best-known of Hitchcock's montage sequences are the shower scene in *Psycho*, the parallel opening in *Shadow of a Doubt*, the staircase escape in *Notorious*, the opening and the runaway carousel climax in *Strangers on a Train*, the United Nations murder in *North by Northwest*, and the crows gathering on the jungle gym in *The Birds*. There are two kinds of montage, editing for an idea and for violence.

EDIT MONTAGE TO CREATE IDEAS

Hitchcock often spoke of the rectangular screen in the movie house to fill, instead of words on a page or on a typewriter. He said that this screen needs to be filled with a succession of images, and the mere fact that they are in sequence is where the ideas come from. In a good montage sequence, the audience isn't aware of the editing of the pictures because they go by so rapidly.

Hitch liked to use an example from a Charlie Chaplin short film called *The Pilgrim* (1923) to demonstrate montage and its importance in creating ideas. "The opening shot was the outside of a prison gate. A guard came out and posted a 'Wanted' notice on a wall. And it's Chaplin in convict clothes. The next shot is a very tall, thin man coming out of a river, having had a swim. He finds that his clothes are missing and have been replaced with a convict's uniform. Next shot, a railroad station, and people waiting for a train, and coming toward the camera dressed with the pants too long is Chaplin. Now there are three pieces of film, and look at the amount of story they told. That's the kind of thing I believe belongs to the cinema."

Hitchcock also spoke of the use of montage in silent Russian films. "It was a possibility of doing a purely cinematic film. You have an immobilized man looking out. That's one part of the film. The second part shows what he sees, and the third part shows how he reacts. This is actually the purest expression of a cinematic idea. Pudovkin dealt with this...In one of his books on the art of montage, he describes an experiment by his teacher, Kuleshov. You see a close-up of the Russian actor Ivan Mosjoukine. This is immediately followed by a shot of a dead baby. Back to Mosjoukine again and you read compassion on his face. Then you take away the dead baby and you show a plate of soup, and now, when you go back to Mosjoukine, he looks hungry. Yet, in both cases, they used the same shot of the actor; his face was exactly the same."

Hitchcock used point of view editing throughout his films, which is all part of his subjective camera technique discussed in Chapter 5. This is putting an idea into the mind of the character without explaining it in dialogue, but done in a point of view shot sequence. You take the eyes of the characters and add something for them to look at.

Start with a close-up of the actor.
Cut to a shot of what they are seeing.
Cut back to the actor to see his reaction.

You can edit back and forth between the character and the subject as many times as you want to build tension; the audience won't get bored. This is the most powerful form of cinema, even more important than acting. To take it even further, have your actor walk toward the subject.

Switch to a tracking shot to show his changing perspective as he walks. The audience will believe that they are sharing something personal with the character. This is what Hitchcock calls "pure cinema" and is a classic trademark from the director.

Rear Window is a fine example of a purely cinematic film. L.B. Jeffries (James Stewart) is wheelchair-bound following an accident at a racetrack. He spends his spare time looking out of his New York apartment, spying on his neighbors. Hitchcock films Stewart looking, one piece of film; the second piece of film is what he sees; the third is his reaction. This is the cinematic motif throughout the film and the three pieces of film represent the purest example of cinematic expression, the juxtaposition of imagery relating to the mind of the individual. You can have the man look, have him see something, have him react in various ways, you can make him look at one thing, another, without him speaking, have his mind at work, comparing things, and it has nothing to do with acting.

As Hitchcock describes pure cinematics, "The assembly of film and how it can be changed to create a different idea... You have a close-up and see what he sees. Let's assume that he sees a woman holding a baby in her arms, and now we cut back to the reaction to what he sees, and he smiles. What is he as a character? He's a kindly old man, he's sympathetic. Now let's take the middle piece of film away, the woman and the child, but leave his two pieces of film as they were, but now put in a piece of film with a girl in a bikini. He looks, girl in a bikini, he smiles, what is he now? He's a dirty old man. He's no longer the benign gentleman who loves babies — that's what film can do."

Hitch would often cut from the close-up not necessarily to get the reaction of the person, although that's part of it, but he wanted to have a reason to cut to what the person is seeing. So a Hitchcock picture looks more open, because he doesn't resort too often to over-the-shoulder

James Stewart in *Rear Window* (1954).

shots. He'll go into a close-up and then you'll see what the person sees. It may be a moving point of view, but he used the point of view as a subjective thing to put the audience within the person. As director John Carpenter says, "Nearest to Alfred Hitchcock's heart was [Sergei] Eisensteinian montage. He used it frequently and adapted its fundamentals in his 'look/see' POV sequences. Hitchcock was darkly funny, obsessed with beautiful icy blondes, and cared most about the audiences who watched his beautifully crafted fables of love and death."

EDIT MONTAGE FOR VIOLENCE AND EMOTION

" The medium of 'pure cinema' is what I believe in. The assembly of pieces of film to create fright is the essential part of my job. Just as

much as a painter might put certain colors together to create evil on canvas. **"** — *Alfred Hitchcock*

The second type of montage is used for editing action and violence sequences. Here the action is edited in a series of close-ups shown in rapid succession. Hitchcock said that editing is best used in violent subjects. He believed that when portraying violence it should be done on the screen in close-up and in montage. Often he gave the example of watching a train pass by: "If you stand in a field and you see a train going by half a mile away, you look at it and it speeds by. Now go within six feet of the train going by and think of the difference in its effect. So what you are doing is you are taking the audience right close-up into the scene, and the montage of the various effects gets the audience involved. That's its purpose. It becomes much more powerful than if you sit back and look. Say you are at a boxing match and you are eight or ten rows back: well, you get a very different effect if you are in the first row, looking up under those ropes."

Bar room brawls in Westerns were always a bore for Hitchcock because they were all shot wide. "If they would only do a few big close-ups here and there, it would be much more exciting, instead of looking at it from a distance," said Hitch.

Editing violence is also best done in succession. This isn't just throwing together random shots into a fight sequence to create confusion, but carefully choosing a close-up of a hand, an arm, a face, a gun falling to the floor, and editing them together to tell a story. In this way you can portray an event by showing various pieces of the action and having careful control over the timing. You can also hide parts of the event so that the mind of the audience is engaged.

Hitchcock believed that it's more effective if such fight scenes are done in montage, because you involve the audience much more. So the basic rule is anytime something important happens, show it in a close-up. Make sure the audience can see it. In *Rear Window,* when Jeffries is thrown out of the window in the end by the villain, Hitchcock just photographed James Stewart's feet, legs, arms, and head, in a complete montage. He also filmed the same sequence from a distance, but the montage is more effective being up close because it involves the emotion much more.

Another example occurs in *North by Northwest* when the heavies rough-up Roger Thornhill. Hitchcock films it in close-up and tight montage. In *Psycho* he directs the audience rather than the actors and is transferring the menace from the screen into the mind of the audience. The famous shower scene in *Psycho* uses montage to hide the violence; you never actually see the knife cutting

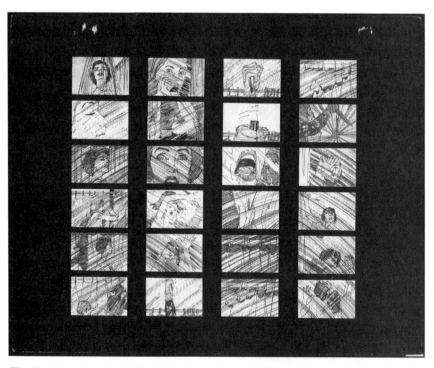

The shower sequence in *Psycho* (1960), storyboard design by Saul Bass.

flesh. The impression of violence is done with quick editing, and the killing takes place inside the viewer's head rather than on the screen.

Psycho contains quite an amount of cinematic content compared to its basic content. As it involved the violent murder of a woman while she takes a shower, Hitch couldn't show a nude woman stabbed to death, so it had to be shown impressionistically, with little pieces of film. "For example, devising in a picture like *Psycho*, the murdering and stabbing of a girl in a shower in a bathroom," said Hitch, "this scene is 45 seconds long, but is made up of 78 pieces of film going through the projector and coming onto the screen in great rapidity. But the overall impression given the audience is one of an alarming, devastating murder scene...My main satisfaction is that film did something to the audience; from a technical viewpoint it could make an audience scream, and create a mass emotion." This is pure cinema, and why he describes *Psycho* as a filmmaker's film.

SAVE YOUR CUTS FOR WHEN YOU NEED THEM

The killing of the detective Arbogast (Martin Balsam) in *Psycho* is another extreme exercise in effective film violence. Hitchcock had storyboards drawn of Arbogast going up the stairs just before he is stabbed to death, as mentioned in the last chapter. One day during filming, Hitchcock was sick and couldn't go to the studio, so he told his AD Hilton Green and assistant Marshall Schlom that they could take the storyboards and shoot them for the detective going up the stairs. There were about 20 shots in the sequence, consisting of feet on the stairs, hand on the rail, close-up, profile, but when Hitchcock looked at it to put together, he thought it was inappropriate, something he had missed in the storyboards.

Hitchcock said, "When I saw them, I said, 'You can't use any of them.'" The sequence told in that way would indicate that the detective was a menace because of the way it was edited. The fast cutting would create suspense. But Hitchcock thought that this is an innocent man; therefore the shot should be innocent. He didn't feel the need to work the audience up. He'd done that. The mere fact that Arbogast is going up the stairs is enough. So he decided to keep it simple with no complications and one continuous shot of him going up the stairs. The shot just needed a simple statement, showing a man going up the stairs in a very simple way, with an air of caution, otherwise the cutting up of the man's journey would ruin the cuts that you needed at the time of his death. So save your edit cuts until you need them.

Editing for violence and montage occurs during the rape and murder of Brenda Blaney (Barbara Leigh-Hunt) in *Frenzy*, combined with a subjective camera, where the scene is played from the point of view of the victim, not Rusk the rapist (played by Barry Foster). Hitchcock starts with a shot of Brenda powdering her nose. She looks up and the man comes through the door. "If you analyze that scene, you'll find that everything is from her point of view," said Hitchcock. "All the fear on her face, the way she tries to head the man off and so forth. Then you only go to the objective, momentarily, when they are so close together, otherwise you just get a nose and eyes on screen because they are so close together. There are moments when you have to switch from the subjective to the objective."

Once Rusk gets Brenda into the chair, Hitchcock goes back to the subjective again, with the man's face leering down on her. He keeps the camera on him: 20 of the 43 shots are tight close-ups of Rusk from Brenda's POV. Brenda is shown in four close-ups from Rusk's point of view — the last shot was used with a filter to soften the image as her struggles cease, but mostly shots taken from under her chin and inserts of her hands that makes us identify with her efforts to break free.

Barbara Leigh-Hunt, who played Brenda, remembers that the scene was shot over three days from 14 different angles to get the small pieces of film Hitchcock needed for the montage, just like the shower scene in *Psycho*. These shots include Brenda's fingers trying to loosen the tie, her head shaking from side to side and then a freeze frame as her eyes suddenly becoming lifeless. A lengthy shot of Rusk and Brenda filmed from the side is cut in with the tie around Brenda's neck.

Many film directors have been influenced by Hitchcock's editing. Joe Carnahan, the director of *Narc* (2002) and *The A-Team* (2010), says "I just loved Hitchcock...I loved *North by Northwest*. *Psycho* is, as much as has been made of that film, it's still amazing how shockingly brutal and violent that movie is, even for a black and white film, you watch that shower scene, man, and it's like, wow, I mean it's really disturbingly graphic and, but again, you're talking about kind of, that's the 'Master' — I mean, that's the guy, he got that, he understood that milieu I think better than anybody ever has, you know."

Editing for violence is effectively used in Martin Scorsese's boxing drama *Raging Bull* (1980), where the shower scene in *Psycho* was used as a template for the fight scenes. The eight fight scenes in *Raging Bull* seem to occupy much of the film, but their total screen time was only ten minutes. The scenes took six weeks to film and even more time was needed to edit the dozens of shots that made up each boxing match. As Scorsese says, "I guess the boxing scenes have a lot to do with the action sequences in my mind. All this editing and all this camera movement that I'd been exposed to for the past 25 years or 30 years came into play in those sequences, and Hitchcock had a lot to do with it, there's no doubt, particularly in designing the scene where Sugar Ray Robinson, in the third bout that they have, when LaMotta's on the ropes, looks up at him, and Sugar Ray comes in for the kill. And there's a kind of edited sequence of punishment that this character's taking. I based it on, shot by shot, the shower scene of *Psycho*. And so I designed it correspondingly, in a way. The glove corresponds to a knife. And so, we shot it that way."

JUMP CUT TO SHOCK

A jump cut is a transition between two shots that appears to jump due to the way the shots are framed in relation to each other. They are usually caused by similar framing and editing out of the continuous action so that the character or object seems to jump between two places. Sometimes a jump cut switches between two actions, cutting between two different times or locales, but uses the same angle and light, cutting from a long shot to a close-up.

Hitchcock uses the jump cut to involve the audience with the characters. *Blackmail* (1929) contains the first example of a jump cut or shock cut when Alice's scream merges with the landlady's discovery of the body. Also, in *The 39 Steps* (1935) there is a famous shock cut from the cleaner's scream to the train whistle. One of the most famous examples of jump cuts can be seen in *The Birds* (1963). Lydia (Jessica Tandy) goes to call on a neighbor and discovers to her horror that birds have killed him. To represent Lydia's point of view, Hitchcock films a triple jump cut, starting with a wide shot of the neighbor's body, a mid shot of his face, and ending with a close-up of his pecked-out eyes. "The three staccato jumps are almost like catching the breath — gasp, gasp, gasp," said Hitch.

A good example of jump cuts can be seen in Tim Burton's *Ed Wood* (1994). Ed is reading an article in a newspaper of an announcement and the camera tightens up on the newspaper to the point where the only thing in the frame is the news article itself. The next shot opens with the same tight shot of the newspaper, but then zooms out and you find that Ed is holding a newspaper in an entirely new location. The jump cut of the location moves the plot along. In the movie *Elizabeth* (1998), when the queen practices her speech, the jump cuts make us feel disoriented and nervous along with the queen, giving us the tension and humor of the situation as if it were a blooper reel.

MATCH CUT TO LINK IDEAS

A match cut is a cut between two different objects in which an object in the two-shots graphically matches. There may be two different spaces, or two different compositions. Match cuts often help to establish a strong continuity of action and link two shots metaphorically.

An effective example of a match occurs at the end of *North by Northwest*, when Roger pulls Eve up from Mount Rushmore, and then Hitchcock cuts to him pulling her up to the top bunk on the train. This match cut speeds through time, skipping over the marriage proposal and marriage. And in *Psycho*, Hitchcock famously uses a match cut after the murder in the shower — the camera shows blood flowing down the plughole of the tub, before match cutting to a shot of Marion's lifeless eye in the same spiral movement.

Other directors have employed match cuts to good effect. In Stanley Kubrick's *2001: A Space Odyssey* (1968), an ape discovers the use of a bone as a tool and throws it up into the air. Kubrick then match cuts thousands of years later to a space vehicle as the modern tool of man, showing his remarkable and rapid evolutionary progress.

CROSS-CUT TO CREATE SUSPENSE

Cross-cutting is the cutting between parallel action, and by rapidly cutting between scenes taking place in different locations, the director can communicate to the audience that the action taking place is simultaneous. Hitchcock used cross-cutting to evoke suspense. Think of a chase scene where a man is being chased by another man. The typical way to evoke suspense is for the director and editor to cross-cut between the man and the man who's chasing him. Or another example, if a man is going to the guillotine, to cross-cut between the man and the executioner. The most common and effective use of cross-cutting is seen in scenes of suspense or horror. In such instances, the protagonist, whom the viewer identifies with, and the threat are presented in tandem. This way, the audience knows information that the protagonist doesn't and finds themselves in a state of anxiety about the plight of the character. By prolonging the time between the meeting of the hero and the threat, this tension can be sustained.

CROSS-CUT FOR CONTRAST

Hitchcock used cross-cutting to compare or contrast two events or characters that seem unrelated. In *Notorious*, Hitchcock cross-cuts between Alicia (Ingrid Bergman) and Devlin (Cary Grant) searching the wine cellar, while upstairs a lavish party is taking place. The cross-cutting also shows close shots of the dwindling supply of champagne upstairs, which creates suspense in the audience, who know that sooner or later someone will go down to the cellar for more. The suspicious Alex (Claude Rains), meanwhile, begins to wonder where his wife has gone. Purely by cinematic editing, Hitchcock creates suspense and tells the story so that by the time Alex goes down to the wine cellar for more champagne, the suspense is unbearable.

Towards the end of *Psycho*, Hitchcock cuts between shots of Lila (Vera Miles) exploring the Bates house and of Sam (John Gavin) trying to divert Norman's (Anthony Perkins) attention in the motel. We realize that Lila is in trouble and needs to get out before Norman finds her. Cross-cutting here increases the tension by delaying knowledge of what is happening at the other space.

WHEN NOT TO CROSS-CUT

Staying with one party and not cross-cutting is a technique that Hitchcock uses to great effect in *The Birds*. Melanie (Tippi Hedren) is seated in front of a schoolhouse smoking, and when she sits down there's a jungle gym behind her and one crow lands on it. The camera is placed on her

The crows gather on the school jungle gym in *The Birds* (1963).

and never shows what's going on behind, until eventually she follows one bird in the sky and when she turns around there's a mass of them waiting to attack. The old technique would have been to cross-cut between the crows gathering of the jungle gym and the smoking Melanie.

When the last crow lands on the climbing frame, the audience discovers the menacing crows at the same time as Melanie. After she goes to warn Annie, the schoolteacher, about the crows gathering outside, Annie devises a plan for the kids to leave the school in a fire drill. Instead of cross-cutting between the children leaving the school and the birds on the jungle gym, Hitchcock's camera now stays with the birds, until the audience hears the patter of the children's feet on the school steps. Someone once asked Hitchcock what happened to the shot of the children going down the steps, and he said there wasn't one — it was all in the audience's minds. That's the power of not cross-cutting.

This device has since become a staple of horror films, and is regularly used when heroines or would-be victims look in the mirror, then pop momentarily out of view, only to find the killer standing behind them and reflected in the mirror when they are seen again.

Cross-cutting can be effectively used for contrast in scenes of action and movement. In *Strangers on a Train*, Hitchcock cross-cuts between Guy's tennis match and Bruno's retrieval of the lighter, followed by the dramatic denouement on a fairground carousel. Guy (Farley Granger) is playing a championship tennis match, knowing that Bruno (Robert Walker) is returning to the fairground, the scene of the murder, with Guy's incriminating cigarette lighter. So Guy must play hard and fast if he is to win the match, get off the court, and catch up with Bruno. Bruno, in the meantime, is confident that Guy is tied up on the tennis court, so he is taking his time and being very leisurely. Hitchcock alternately cuts from Guy's frenzied movements to Bruno's controlled pace, creating a kind of counterpoint between two kinds of movement — one hurried, the other leisurely. And at the climax of the film, cross-cutting is superbly employed to cut between an old man crawling under the carousel, a fight between Guy and Bruno, and the carousel horses spinning out of control.

Cross-cutting can also be used to bring out a darker reality below the surface: for example, in Francis Coppola's *The Godfather* (1972) between a Mafia wedding and planting a dead horse in an enemy's bed; and in Bob Fosse's *Cabaret* (1972) between a decadent stage show and a violent Nazi beating.

In *United 93* (2006), director Paul Greengrass uses parallel cutting throughout to differentiate between the terrorists, unsuspecting passengers, and the flight crew of United 93 as they prepare to take off from Newark to San Francisco on September 11, 2001. Greengrass uses an edgy, *cinéma vérité* style that disorients the audience. He creates tension by cutting between unsuspecting innocent passengers, the terrorists, and the people on the ground.

USE SHOT LENGTH TO INCREASE SUSPENSE

Hitchcock used the length of each shot to create his suspense and drama and shot lengths are often indicative of the subject's feelings about the present. In *Shadow of a Doubt*, Hitchcock used shot length to great effect when Charlie (Teresa Wright) goes to the library up until the point where she finds the truth about her uncle. The first three shots are about the same length — they are all moderately long. Hitchcock purposely made these three shots longer to juxtapose the shortness of the shots that are to follow. The rhythm of this sequence changes after shot #4 when Charlie tries to cross the street; the shots become very short and quick. As the shots get shorter and the cutting more rapid, the audience experiences the same feelings as Charlie; her anxious desire to get to the library before it closes, her shock after almost being hit by a passing car, and her impatience at the pedestrian crossing.

In *North by Northwest*, during the attack on Thornhill by the crop-duster plane, Hitchcock kept the shots between the attacks deliberately long to prepare the audience for the threat of each dive of the plane. The length of the shots was also used to indicate the various distances that Thornhill had to run for cover and to show that there was no cover he could go to. It was necessary for Hitchcock to show the full approach of the plane because it goes by so fast, and if the shots were too fast, then the plane is in and out of the shot so quickly that the audience is not aware of it.

Like the crop-duster scenes, Hitchcock varies the length of the bird attack shots in *The Birds*. In some of the gull attacks in the children's birthday party, longer shots of the gulls coming down were needed. In theory, you shouldn't show that, because they attack a person before they are aware of it. For example, when the first gull attacks Melanie in the boat, the scene starts off being subjective. Melanie is watching a car, and the dockside, and then something suddenly hits her. Hitchcock knew you have to break a rule there and show the gull before it hits her, so you have to leave the subjective and go to the objective so the audience is aware of what is happening, which lengthens the shot.

In the scene when Scottie drags Judy up the bell tower at the end of *Vertigo*, Hitchcock was very specific about the timing of each of the shots. "Going up the stairs, we worked out the length of the shots with the metronome, so we were getting the rhythm of going up the stairs as he wanted, that was very important to him," remembers

Kim Novak. "Hitchcock wanted us to hit our marks and edited the sequence precisely."

FAST CUTTING

Hitchcock's films are noted for their fast cutting, as can be seen in classic sequences in *Psycho* and *Frenzy*. Even in his early film *Sabotage* (1936), Hitchcock cuts to a different angle of the bomb every time to give it a vitality, to say 'this is a live bomb,' so that the audience doesn't get used to it. "I did that to give the bomb a vitality of its own, to animate it," he said. "If I'd shown it constantly from the same angle, the public would have become used to the package: 'Oh well, it's only a package, after all.' But what I was saying was 'Be careful! Watch out!'"

As already mentioned, there were about 43 shots in *Frenzy*'s strangulation. The sequence is noted for the fast cutting, and as Hitchcock says, "That is the whole point. You suggest violence by the rapidity of the cuts." The potato truck sequence alone had 118 shots and to help the editor, Hitchcock had a special number for each shot, "Because I realized the cutter would be confronted with a whole lot of film — close-ups of the killer and potato sacks behind him, and he would get awfully confused which was which. So I had special numbers made. Yellow cards with black figures in them, and each shot was numbered accordingly to my dictated sheet."

When Hitchcock was working in Hollywood, films typically contained between 300 and 700 shots, giving them an average shot length of 8 to 11 seconds. But by the 1980s, the average shot length was 5 seconds as fast cutting was used for action sequences, such as chases, fights, and gunplay. But even in dialogue scenes the cutting is more rapid and non-action films can also be very fast-cut.

Fast cutting has become an almost gratuitous effect as entire films use the technique in an attempt to make the films high-powered without relying on superior storytelling. There are still many skillful examples of fast cutting, such as the famous chase scene in *The French Connection* (1971), and in *The Bourne Ultimatum* (2007), where the average shot length in the action sequences is 2 seconds. When you combine that fast editing style with "shaky cam" shooting, it's too much for some audiences. Film critic Roger Ebert received so many letters about the editing style of the *Bourne* movies that he published them in his column entitled "The Shaky-Queasy-Ultimatum."

GRAPHICS AND OPENING TITLES

As Hitchcock was a visual artist who trained as a designer of intertitles for silent films, he had a very keen visual sense for the value of strong title and poster designs. He was constantly trying to think of fresh ideas and admitted to getting into elaborate tricks when doing so. Moving from Britain to America, he saw movie titles as being much more advanced and was able, with the help of collaborators such as the graphic designer Saul Bass, to come up with various innovative opening titles that established the film's theme, era, style, and tone of narrative.

In his collaboration with Saul Bass, Hitch achieved a brilliant orchestration of graphics, text, and music, from *Vertigo* through to *North by Northwest* and *Psycho*. *Vertigo* begins with the close-up of a woman's eye. The lines shift and stretch to create a multitude of eye-like forms, creating a hypnotic sequences that establishes the mood of the film as a powerful psychological thriller.

Psycho's titles of horizontal and vertical bars replicates the visual composition of the movie, which is preceded in the opening image of the tall skyscrapers, the standing John Gavin over the horizontal Janet Leigh, and then by the Bates house towering over the horizontal Bates Motel. The fragmented bars of the opening titles represent knife slashes and Norman Bates' damaged psyche.

The Birds starts with the eerie and menacing image of birds across the screen, as Hitchcock knew that the audience would be impatient to see the birds from the start. Originally he was going to begin the film with delicate Chinese drawings of birds, but he abandoned this idea for the more potent and frightening image of birds flying across the screen.

Saul Bass' titles for Hitchcock have influenced many other title designers such as Pablo Ferro, whose work includes *Dr. Strangelove* (1964), *A Clockwork Orange* (1971), and *L.A. Confidential* (1997). Bass' look appears on screen in the opening credits for such Martin Scorsese films as *Cape Fear* (1991), with its threatening patterns of light on disturbed water, and *The Age of Innocence* (1993), with its beautiful but menacing roses. Kyle Cooper's scratchy jump cut credits for *Se7en* (1995) look as if they could have been etched out by the film's serial killer. The candy-colored animation for Steven Spielberg's *Catch Me If You Can* (2002) is a Bass poster come to life, with retro font and graphics and a jazzy theme tune.

Pedro Almodóvar's *Bad Education* (2004) has striking similarities to *Vertigo*. Both films open with credit sequences complete with frantic strings and stylized graphics. The score from *Bad Education* sounds inspired by Bernard Herrmann's score for *Vertigo*. The stylized ripping graphics that characterize *Bad Education*'s opening also evoke the kind of movement and imagery Saul Bass provided for *Vertigo*.

In *Broken Embraces* (2009) Almodóvar uses bold colors and performances that are real and piercing, creating Hitchcockian suspense at times, in scenes that call to mind *Notorious*. *The Skin I Live In* (2011) is a story about a mad doctor who is trying to physically transform someone into a perfect copy of his dead wife. Thematically it's similar to Hitchcock's *Vertigo*, as well as the French horror movie *Eyes Without a Face* (1960). Almodóvar says, "As far as *Vertigo* goes, you're always going to be quoting Hitchcock if you're telling the story of a man creating a new woman in the image of another dead woman."

THE OPENING

"A good film should start with an earthquake and be followed by rising tension." — *Alfred Hitchcock*

Hitchcock's films are full of memorable openings. Some start with suspenseful action sequences, others suggest the location. The first shot of *Vertigo* begins with a horizontal bar. The camera pulls back to reveal that it's the rung of a ladder, and immediately we're into the start of an exciting chase sequence, as detective Scottie Ferguson pursues a criminal across the San Francisco rooftops at night. Moments later he slips and experiences terrible vertigo, and subsequently feels responsible for the death of the police officer who falls trying to help him.

Baz Luhrmann, the director of *Moulin Rouge!* (2001), *Australia* (2008), and *The Great Gatsby* (2013), says that the opening three minutes of *Vertigo* are "some of the most thrilling in any movie ever...the first ever use of the *Vertigo* Shot, the background receding rapidly, back to the look of horror on Jimmy's face...a perfectly structured three minutes."

In *Psycho* the camera starts with a high aerial shot of Phoenix, Arizona, spelling out the exact day and time — Friday December 11 2:43 p.m. — before tracking into the window of a high-rise building. The camera tracks through the window and we eavesdrop on two lovers after a tryst of lunchtime sex. Immediately the voyeur theme of the movie is established. This aerial shot was done before the advent of Tyler mounts or helicopter shots, said *Psycho* script supervisor Marshall Schlom.

The opening of *The Birds* is memorable and menacing, showing everyday city life as the chic Melanie Daniels crosses Union Square in San Francisco while ominous flocks of seagulls gather in the sky above. Hitchcock said that his film was about complacency and how people take nature for granted, although at any moment chaos can erupt.

In *Marnie* the camera tracks on a bulging yellow handbag, which the viewer soon learns contains almost $10,000 in stolen cash. It also establishes the corridor and journey motif of Marnie as she walks along the platform into the distance. All of these openings in Hitchcock's movies state the theme of the movie with economy and simplicity.

THE ENDING

A good film has an ending that answers the beginning and *The 39 Steps* is a classic case of this. The film opens in a music hall and ends in the London Palladium, each with the character of "Mr. Memory" entertaining an audience and both ending in the firing of a gun.

Other films neatly mirror the beginning and the end. *Vertigo* ends on the desolate image of Scottie at the top of the bell tower, having finally conquered the fear of heights that first strikes him at the film's opening, but having just once again lost the woman he loved. "It's just as well that Judy did die, because where could it go if she didn't? There would be no peace of mind between her and Scottie," says Kim Novak.

The frightening grin of Norman Bates closes *Psycho* (a shot in which Hitchcock superimposes Mrs. Bates' skull over Anthony Perkins' face for added effect), but then Hitch adds a final shot of Marion's car being pulled out of the swamp. In this way, Hitchcock reminds us of the person we first met at the film's start — the doomed embezzler Marion Crane — whose dead body is contained in the car's trunk.

Hitchcock often wrapped up his films quickly, calling any additional scenes "Hat Grabbers." He reasoned that the audience would be grabbing for their hat and filing out of the movie theatres because in their minds the film was over. The ending of *North by Northwest* is wrapped up in 45 seconds. From Roger holding onto Eve for dear life over Mount Rushmore, Hitchcock cuts to him pulling her up to the top berth of the 20th Century Limited train, with the words "Come along, Mrs. Thornhill." This perfect economy brings together the film's themes of resistance to marriage.

Sometimes the ending is unresolved, as in the case of *The Birds*, when the birds have taken over Bodega Bay, forcing the Brenner family to flee in Melanie's convertible. But flee to what? Hitchcock kept the ending open.

EXERCISES

1. Take an action scene in your movie. Break it down into individual shots and number how you will edit them together in a montage sequence. What is the overall effect?

2. In a chase or suspense sequence, show how staying with one character instead of cross-cutting can enhance the suspense.

3. Watch the shower sequence in *Psycho*. Can you see if the knife ever actually strikes the victim?

4. In *Rear Window*, how is L.B. Jeffries' act of looking out of the window across the courtyard similar to our act of watching a film?

Key Hitchcock films to watch

Rear Window (1954)
Psycho (1960)
The Birds (1964)

Other directors' films to watch

Cape Fear (1991)
Se7en (1995)
The *Bourne* films

Further reading

In the Blink of an Eye (2001) by Walter Murch

CHAPTER SEVEN

SOUND AND MUSIC

"I think what sound brought of value to the cinema was to complete the realism of the image on the screen. It made everyone in the audience deaf mutes. **"** *— Alfred Hitchcock*

Think of a Hitchcock movie and you immediately think of wonderful visuals accompanied by an evocative soundtrack. Over the course of his career, Hitchcock employed more styles and techniques than any other director in film history, and experimented with and was sensitive to all kinds of sounds — natural, mechanical, musical — as well as to silence. His innovations span the history of cinema, from silent films to the first talkies. Sound was used as part of his artistic technique to put the audience through it.

He used subliminal sound in *Secret Agent*, distorted dialogue in *Blackmail*, effective use of silence in *Frenzy*, and he pioneered electronic sound effects in *The Birds*. He used interior monologues in *Murder* and also in *Psycho* when Marion is driving her car to California after stealing the money. Hitchcock wove

Scottie (James Stewart) and
Madeleine (Kim Novak) kiss,
accompanied by the haunting
music of Bernard Herrmann's
score, in *Vertigo* (1958).

music and musicians frequently into his plots, and some
of Hitchcock's finest sequences have memorable music.
There's the sad, romantic music for *Vertigo*, the exhila-
rating score for *North by Northwest*, and the screaming
violins in *Psycho*. More than half of his films include
music as an essential part of the plot, and eight of his
characters are musicians. Some of his characters become
obsessed with music so that it becomes a clue to the drama.
The characters in *The 39 Steps, The Lady Vanishes*, and
Shadow of a Doubt are all haunted by pieces of music,
such as the tune that Hannay can't quite get out of his
head in *The 39 Steps* and the melody carried by Miss Froy
in *The Lady Vanishes*, which turns out to be a vital clause
of a secret pact between two European countries.

UTILIZE SILENCE FOR EFFECT

Hitchcock knew that silence was often as effective as
music and it could be heightened by using music just

before or after it. He once said, "If it's a good movie, the sound could go off and the audience would still have a perfectly clear idea of what was going on."

In *Rebecca* (1940) Hitchcock almost never showed Mrs. Danvers (Judith Anderson) walking into a room where Joan Fontaine's character was. Fontaine would always hear a sound and then see Mrs. Danvers standing perfectly still by her side. Hitchcock explained, "I felt that I had to treat it from the girl's point of view. To see her walk into that position would be humanizing her." He effectively used silence in Mrs. Danvers' scenes to convey her supernatural-like quality.

In *Saboteur* (1942), at the top of the Statue of Liberty, Hitchcock didn't use music, just the sound effects of the wind. "Remoteness, above everything, just wind," was the effect he was trying to achieve. In *Notorious* (1946) there are also many silent scenes as Alicia is slowly poisoned by Alex and his mother, because Hitchcock wanted to convey a silent, methodical murder.

In *Frenzy* (1972), silence is effectively and memorably used in the murder of Babs the barmaid. When she quits her job at the pub, Babs runs into Rusk, whom she doesn't know is the necktie murderer. Hitchcock eliminates all noise on the soundtrack except Rusk's words: "Got a place to stay?" As Hitchcock instructed in his cutting notes, "When she comes to 'big head' [close-up], drop all sounds — traffic and everything. And bring it up again when the camera tracks back to the two-shot of Rusk and Babs so we get the effect when his voice is heard behind her 'big head' there is no sound whatsoever. This is dramatic license but I think it is necessary to get the fullest effect of Rusk's sudden appearance." The effect, as Hitchcock said, was "chilling."

With Babs' murder, Hitchcock preferred to let the audience use their imagination. We have just witnessed the brutal rape and murder of Brenda, so we don't need to see another explicit murder. Hitchcock suggested, "Why don't we just have the murderer take her up to his apartment, open the door for her and say 'You're my kind of woman,' and close the door. We know exactly what is happening behind that closed door. The camera retreats down a narrow, twisting staircase along the hallway and out into the street."

Hitchcock put the camera on a crane which glided silently back down the stairs, and then out the front door onto the noisy London street. "And I think it's a fairly well-known cinema trick," Hitch said. "In the studio, we had the stairway built. The U-shaped stairway, and with a railway for the cradle...with the operator and the camera sitting in the cradle so that he's coming down and 'round the U and back down the stairs, along the hallway, and as the camera clears the lintel of the front door, which was built in the studio, an extra dressed like a Covent Garden porter with a huge sack of potatoes wipes the screen. Go out to location in Tavistock Street, have the man walk across and wipe the screen with the potato sack and track back. Cue pedestrians, cue the cyclists, cue the cars, and it seems to be an uninterrupted sequence."

Once outside, Hitchcock increased the traffic noise up to a tremendous roar, as his cutting notes describe, "And now exaggerate all the traffic noise as we pull back to show the façade of the building — and make it almost a roar of traffic — louder than it would normally be." The audience subconsciously says, "Well if she screams, she's never going to be heard." The silence becomes horrifying as the audience imagines the murder taking place inside.

SOUND EFFECTS

"Like cuts, sound effects should be in one's mind before one starts the picture so they can be incorporated into the script and included as we go along." — Alfred Hitchcock

As much as Hitchcock enjoyed silence, he looked forward to the advent of sound. He knew that careful use of sound can help strengthen the intensity of the situation, and believed that there should be sound effects of some kind throughout the whole film. He also knew that if the sound effects dropped suddenly, then the film tends to drop with it, as it appears to be a break in continuity.

What Hitchcock never tended to do was tone down sound to suit the convenience of the story. For example, if he was filming in a factory, he would never dim the roar of the machines so that an actor could be heard distinctly making wisecracks.

In *Rear Window*, Hitchcock used sparing, precise sounds and source music to create the atmosphere of the Greenwich Village courtyard in which the story takes place. The score is a soundtrack from the various apartments, for example, when a neighbor is playing music across the way, maybe on the radio, or another neighbor is listening to a record or a man is playing the piano. Other than that, there was no score in *Rear Window*, which was a very unusual, and at that time, a rather daring thing to do.

Hitchcock prepared a detailed sound list and was actively involved in the creation of the soundtrack. In *Psycho*, he needed the sound of a knife going into someone's flesh, so he did a blind sound test among different types of melons, finally settling on a casaba. He said to the prop man, "bring me a casaba melon and a knife, that's what we'll use." He plunged the knife into the melon. He knew about sound effects and 99% of the time, these were listed on paper and in the script.

In *The Birds* Hitchcock went on to experiment in even more daring ways as there is no musical score, but just the electronic score of bird cries. In the final scene, he uses an electronic hum, which Hitchcock described as the purr of a car engine, as the birds lull between their attacks. During the making of that film Hitchcock and composer Bernard Herrmann used an instrument called a trautonium, which pioneered electronic sound.

Sound is also effectively used in the pursuit through the East Berlin Museum in *Torn Curtain*. Professor Michael Armstrong (Paul Newman) pretends to defect to the East, and is chased through the museum by an unseen follower. All he and the audience hear is the tapping of shoes on the marble floor. The narrative is underscored not by a suspenseful soundtrack, but by the minimalist tapping of two pairs of shoes.

Today's directors attuned to the expressive potential of sound include Michael Haneke. *Caché* (2005) is about a Parisian couple (played by Daniel Auteuil and Juliette Binoche) who are spied upon using a hidden digital camera. Haneke doesn't utilize a conventional soundtrack and none of the characters are seen listening to music. Instead, natural sounds are used, such as screeching tires, car doors slamming, footsteps on the pavement, and ringing doorbells. This encourages the audience to engage in the film by listening to these background noises to try and solve the mystery of the story.

AMBIENT SOUND

"Motion pictures were driven into the studios by sound. Until sound they had always been made in the open. I prefer shooting on location because it enables you to utilize atmosphere."
— *Alfred Hitchcock*

Ambient sound is any sound that is part of a location. Take, for example, a train station. The ambient sounds will include the whine of train brakes, the sounds of arrival and departure announcements, and the general noise of people walking and talking.

Hitchcock makes great use of ambient sound in *Rear Window.* What's interesting is how he filmed the shots in order to the get the sound quality that he needed. Hitch actually shot live sound from Jeffries' point of view to capture the genuine hollow sound between the window where he was sitting and the various apartments across the courtyard.

Another clever use of ambient sound occurs when one of Stewart's neighbors discovers that her dog has been murdered. Hitchcock has the woman cry out and all the neighbors come to listen, except Thorwald the murderer. It's a very evocative scene and becomes an important clue to Jeffries and Lisa and makes them convinced that Thorwald is guilty. The human imagination is far more sinister than anything that could be produced on screen. During the memorable moment when Mrs. Thorwald is murdered, only the sound of her scream can be heard in the background.

In *The Man Who Knew Too Much,* Hitchcock uses sound and music as a powerful suspense device. Earlier, before the attempted assassination at the Albert Hall, Hitchcock plays for the assassin (and the audience), the sound of the clash of symbols that will disguise the fatal gunshot. As Hitchcock says, he derived the idea of a musical cue from "the suspense of the little man waiting to play his one note, that gave me the idea of the suspense when he goes up to pick up those cymbals." The rehearsal with the record was played so that the audience would know what the sound was like. The audience knew what to expect and when it should come musically, to provide them with

Alfred Hitchcock and Bernard Herrmann on the set of *The Man Who Knew Too Much* (1956).

the idea, so there is no confusion. This goes back to the old rule of giving the audience information.

Hitchcock can find something healthy in a scream and something sinister in laughter. In both versions of *The Man Who Knew Too Much*, a scream saves a life. At the end of *Rear Window*, when Jeffries is hanging out of the window, his cries for help finally acknowledges his dependence on others as he shouts "Lisa! Doyle!" — especially his previous resistance to girlfriend Lisa.

In *North by Northwest*, during the crop-duster sequence Hitchcock uses naturalistic sound effects, dominated by the buzz of the aircraft, which greatly contributes to the tension as it dive bombs Roger Thornhill. Only when the plane hits the truck and explodes does Hitchcock use Herrmann's music with a rousing, ironic fanfare. For Hitchcock, "a rest could be as significant as a note."

DIALOGUE

Hitchcock started his career making silent films, so he was famously distrustful of dialogue and even complained in the late 1920s about the arrival of the so-called "talkies." Dialogue, he felt, was a stage device, whereas films were primarily visual and he objected to films that were merely photographs of people talking.

Blackmail (1929) was a landmark "talkie" with effective use of sound, such as the much-celebrated sequence at the breakfast table. The girl Alice, played by Anny Ondra, has just committed a murder with a knife the night before, and is sitting at breakfast with her parents. A talkative neighbor arrives from next door and starts gossiping about the murder and what a terrible thing it is to kill a man in the back with a knife. As the woman rambles, the dialogue gets fuzzier and fuzzier except for the repeated word "knife." Hitchcock keeps the camera close on Alice's face, while in the background all that can be heard from the neighbor is the word "knife, knife, knife" continuously jumping out from the soundtrack. Suddenly the voice of the father says, "Pass the bread knife will you Alice?" Alice reaches for the knife, but is so shocked at the word "knife" that it jumps out of her hand. It's a very effective and innovative use of dialogue from Hitchcock's first talkie.

Blackmail interestingly started out as a silent film, but switched to sound during the course of the production. "In fact, while I was shooting it as a silent picture, they told me that the last reel was going to be done in sound," said Hitchcock. This was Hitchcock's first experiment with sound, and led to many of his films featuring as little dialogue as was possible.

Originally dialogue was planned for the scene when Ben (James Stewart) chases Jo (Doris Day) up the stairs of the Albert Hall in *The Man Who Knew Too Much*. The dialogue was supposed to have a great deal of exposition that cleared up many of the plot points. But just before shooting, Hitchcock decided to abandon the dialogue and said to Stewart, "Just follow Doris up the stairs and look tense." The dialogue isn't missed in the final cut, and the scene is very effective with just Bernard Herrmann's rousing music.

USE SONGS DRAMATICALLY

"If you've got a singer, use it dramatically. You don't just shove her into singing. You can't do that. " — *Alfred Hitchcock*

The Lady Vanishes, Rear Window, The Man Who Knew Too Much, The Birds, and *Marnie* all have songs woven into the storyline that are part of the plot. Hitchcock stripped musical scores and used singing and whistling as suspense devices in *The Man Who Knew Too Much.*

In *The Lady Vanishes,* the secrets Miss Froy (Dame May Whitty) has memorized are in the form of a tune that she must sing to be decoded. So a simple melody turns out to have a significant role in the plot. When Michael Redgrave's character, Gilbert, a musicologist, forgets the melody, it's up to Miss Froy to remember it.

In *Rear Window,* a recurring theme is the song "Lisa" that a songwriter in one of the other apartments is struggling to compose. The song becomes an integral part of the development of the story as its pieced together over the course of the movie. When it's finally heard complete, a suicidal neighbor, "Miss Lonelyhearts," is so inspired by it that she decides not to commit suicide as planned.

Sound designer Gary Rydstrom, who has edited films such as *Saving Private Ryan* (1999) and *Minority Report* (2002), says of *Rear Window,* "So now we come to the end of the movie, and visual, this is a scene about Grace Kelly. Jimmy Stewart has wondered, you know, 'Is she the girl

Jeffries (James Stewart) and Lisa (Grace Kelly) listen to a neighbor's song as it's being composed in *Rear Window* (1954).

for me? She's a Park Avenue girl. Is she tough enough for me?' She breaks into Raymond Burr's apartment, you know, the bad guy's apartment, when he's not there, to get a clue. From here on it's just that song, which is called 'Lisa.' This is the fullest expression of the song we've heard in the movie so far, the most complete version of the song that represents their love story. But what's happening is that Hitchcock is showing us the part of the movie that's a murder mystery. This is really suspenseful and painful to watch. The soundtrack is climaxing the love story, because the song is telling us that Jimmy Stewart is now finally in love with Grace Kelly. But the disconnect is rich. If you have the soundtrack telling you one part of the story, and the visuals telling you another, there's this richness that comes out of it, as well as a tension because the mood of the music is not the mood of what we're seeing."

Hitchcock also uses song as an integral part of the plot in *The Man Who Knew Too Much*. Hitchcock, of course, knew about Doris Day's fame as a singer, and that the audience watching would expect her to sing. But rather than asking Day to sing for no particular reason, Hitchcock cleverly integrated a song so that it becomes a crucial part of the movie.

In an early scene in their Moroccan hotel, Day's character, Jo, sings to her son while she is putting him to bed. (When asked what she thought of the song, Day said, "I thought it was a little song, I didn't think about it. I knew that it was good for the plot." That "little song" — "Que Sera Sera (Whatever Will Be Will Be)" — became one of Day's biggest successes and won that year's Oscar for Best Original Song.)

Later in the film's plot, Jo must sing "Que Sera Sera" again in order to catch the attention of her son, who's being held by kidnappers somewhere in the same

Doris Day and Christopher Olsen perform "Que Sera Sera" in *The Man Who Knew Too Much* (1956).

building. Hitchcock, thereby, turns the very act of singing into suspense.

Since Hitchcock loved contrast, he effectively used counterpoint sounds and music to lull the viewer into a false sense of security. In *The Birds*, a children's song is used to extend the suspense sequence as the crows gather behind Melanie on the jungle gym, and in fact screenwriter Evan Hunter was asked to extend the song with several verses just to keep the suspense going. Whereas in *Marnie*, the song that the children sing outside Marnie's mother's house, "Mother, Mother, I am ill, send for the doctor over the hill," is a reflection of Marnie's mental state and illness.

MUSIC

"Music's appeal is to a great extent emotional...
To neglect music, I think, is to surrender,
willfully or not, a chance of progress in film-
making" — Alfred Hitchcock

Film music and editing have a great deal in common, and Hitchcock had an understanding that some of the most powerful effects are created not so much by what you see but what you hear. Music provides the emotion that makes you understand what the characters feel and makes you forget being a passive spectator, drawing you into the story and making you emotionally involved. The purpose of both music and editing includes creating the tempo and mood of the scene.

Composer Bernard Herrmann memorably scored seven films for Hitchcock: *The Trouble With Harry* (1955), *The Man Who Knew Too Much* (1956), *The Wrong Man* (1957), *Vertigo* (1958), *North by Northwest* (1959), *Psycho* (1960), and *Marnie* (1964), and he supervised the electronic score for *The Birds* (1963). Many deem the Hitchcock-Herrmann partnership as one of the greatest director-composer partnerships in film history.

Hitchcock famously said, "I think music is very good, especially when it is needed for silence." He believed that a film should have a complete score, but not a continuous one. Whereas silence was very effective, its effect is heightened by the proper handling of music before and after.

MUSIC FOR ATMOSPHERE

The first and obvious use of music is atmospheric, to create excitement and intensity. The basis of the cinema's appeal is emotional and music's appeal is to a great extent emotional as well. In a scene of action, for instance, when the aim is to build up to a physical climax, music adds excitement just as effectively as cutting. Music can also be a background to a scene in any mood and a commentary on dialogue.

Just as the ideal editing is the kind you don't notice as editing, so too it is with music. Hitchcock said, "I've always found with musicians that you're in their hands anyway. What can you do? So very often, I've been asked — not necessarily by Mr. Herrmann, but by other musicians — they say, 'Come down, I want to know what you think of this.' You go down and you say, 'I don't care for it' [and they say] 'Well you can't change it; it's all scored.' So the next time you take care and you say, 'Can you play me some and let me hear some before you go to the expense of an orchestra?' [and they say] 'Oh no no. You can't play it on a piano. It's not possible.' So there is no way to find out. So you are in the hands of a musician."

MUSIC FOR EMOTION

The second use of music is to create emotion. Hitchcock used music psychologically in tune with his characters. A great score delves into the mental or psychological state of the characters, rather than just commenting on their physical action. As an editor it's important to consider the rhythm as the film is cut between dialogue and cuts between shots.

One of the most famous pieces of music in Hitchcock's films is Bernard Herrmann's score for the shower scene in *Psycho*. Music contributes immensely to the sequence. The shower scene is a masterpiece of suspense and shock — the way the visual is cut with the discordant, rapid string movements of Herrmann's legendary score that suggests screams of pain and the slashing of a knife.

Originally Hitchcock didn't want music for the scene, but just the sound of the knife and the running water. He was downbeat about the scene when he first saw it. But when Herrmann, who went against Hitchcock's wishes and composed a score for the shower scene, played it to him, Hitchcock was convinced that music added immeasurably to the violence. Herrmann used a string orchestra rather than a full orchestra for *Psycho*, thus limiting his range of musical colors. A black and white score to match the black and white picture.

Equally memorable is Herrmann's music when Marion is driving from Phoenix to Fairvale with the stolen money. Herrmann says of this justifiably celebrated sequence — "My music tells you what she is thinking." The scene is cut between only three shots: one of Janet Leigh driving in close-up, one of her view of the road, and one of the police in the rearview mirror. It's gripping because of Bernard Herrmann's score. We empathize with Marion and don't want her to get caught.

MUSIC FOR COUNTERPOINT

"Murder can be fun." — *Alfred Hitchcock*

Hitchcock also liked to use counterpoint music, where the music is in juxtaposition to what's on screen or is about to be shown on screen. He famously said to the composer John Williams during the scoring of *Family Plot*, "Mr.

Williams, murder can be fun." For Hitchcock there was irony and many sides to the prism of what one sees in relation to what one hears.

Frenzy starts with light woodwinds and glockenspiels to match the sparkling daylight, and has one of the most majestic openings in Hitchcock's films. An aerial view of the River Thames in London slowly tracks towards Tower Bridge in the distance, all set to Ron Goodwin's score. Originally Henry Mancini was hired to compose the score, but he received no specific instructions, so he constructed a dark, foreboding score typical of Herrmann. Hitchcock, who loved contrast, had other thoughts and wanted to lull the viewer into a false sense of security. So he was very specific with his instructions to Goodwin. Later Mancini ruefully said that he wished he had been given the same directions when composing his score.

Another use of counterpoint music occurs in *Topaz*. The Russian girl Tamara, who has defected with her family to the West, is playing a classical melody while the agents are arguing downstairs. Hitchcock noted at the time: "Music should have grace and simplicity to counterpoint the argument downstairs. Needn't necessarily be Russian, which might be too obvious."

Hitchcock and Herrmann's relationship is mirrored later by the collaboration of Steven Spielberg and John Williams. In *Jaws* (1975) Williams' smooth, rapid, bass-heavy string scoring embodies the speed, power, and movement of the great white shark underwater. 30 years later, Spielberg's film *Munich* (2005) also uses a similar but much more understated score from Williams, with rapidly accelerating electric bass notes, used to ratchet up the tension immediately prior to each assassination attempt by the Israeli hit squad.

Other celebrated composer-director combinations include Henry Mancini and Blake Edwards, James Newton Howard and M. Night Shyamalan, Danny Elfman and Tim

Burton, Nina Rota and Federico Fellini, Ennio Morricone and Sergio Leone, and Hans Zimmer and Ridley Scott. Paul Hirsch is an editor whose film credits include *Star Wars* (1977), *Ferris Bueller's Day Off* (1986), and more recently *Source Code* (2010) and *Mission: Impossible – Ghost Protocol* (2011). *Psycho* was very inspirational to him and he used a cue from *Psycho* in *Star Wars*, when they are searching the Millennium Falcon; the music that he used was a famous three-note motif, which was an homage to Herrmann.

Other works referencing Bernard Herrmann include Danny Elfman's titles and music for *Spider-Man* (2002), and *The Fugitive* (1992) by James Newton Howard, who's marching bands camouflage the wrong man hero. *Signs* (2002), directed by M. Night Shyamalan and composed by James Newton Howard, also evokes Herrmann's music. This is particularly evident in the opening titles sequence — in which the credit and title cards are accompanied by dissonant music that gives the audience a sense of the horror to come later in the film. The silences in *Signs* have an enormous amount of tension, which is partly charged by the music, including the opening title music. So Shyamalan, like Hitchcock, effectively counterpoints music with silence.

The score of Martin Scorsese's *Shutter Island* (2010) also evokes Herrmann. Scorsese used existing music only, compiled by himself and music supervisor Robbie Robertson. "Robbie Robertson came up with this idea of modern symphonic music. He started sending me CDs and went ahead with demanding Ingram Marshall, John Adams." This is an extreme example of a director exerting authorial control over the music, where the composer is not even included, but rather the director and music supervisor are able to choose existing music that might work with the film, try it against the picture, and then pay to use it. This approach of using existing music for greater control started with Kubrick's *2001: A Space Odyssey* (1968) and is even more easy with today's digital revolution.

Alexandre Desplat, who composed the sweeping musical score to Roman Polanski's *The Ghost Writer* (2010), was also inspired by Herrmann. His score is filled with nuance and subtlety, and breathes tension into moments that propel the tension forward as we follow the main character's Hitchcockian investigation into what's really going on around the embattled former Prime Minister. Polanski balances emotional weight with silence, just as Hitchcock often did, and Desplat's score skillfully uses themes to increase suspense and emotion.

Desplat also incorporates many ambient sounds like car horns and clanking iron into his score, and uses this as a resounding motif, producing a melodic sequence that uses the rise and fall of foghorns to accentuate the sense of danger. The similarities with Bernard Herrmann's scores are obvious. In *Vertigo*, Herrmann incorporates a foghorn's call for danger in his score. Desplat admits to being inspired by Herrmann: "As much as I admire Herrmann's sense of energy and lyricism, I prefer his very restrained passages with pure lines, like in Hitchcock's *North by Northwest*, or his lesser-known works, like *The Ghost and Mrs. Muir*."

SPOTTING MUSIC

After a film was edited, Hitchcock dictated what he called "a reel sound script" to his secretary. Every part of the film was run off and Hitch indicated all the places where sounds should be heard, and places where there should be silence. He also noted the places where music would enhance what's being played on the screen. Creating the soundtrack is one of the most collaborative parts of filmmaking, as it involves the director, editor, and assistants.

Decisions about the amount of music come under the umbrella of "spotting." Spotting is the art of choosing where and where *not* to have music in a film, and what kind of music and for what purpose. Spotting decisions are usually given from the director to the composer at the spotting meeting. In fact, spotting decisions are among the only music-related decisions that Hitchcock could actually claim as his own, apart from the decision to hire or fire a composer. The rest would more accurately be attributed to his composer. The only time Hitchcock ever heard some themes played before the movie was scored was on *Spellbound* and *Topaz*.

Composer John Williams vividly remembers one instance of spotting during the scoring of *Family Plot*. There was a room where the criminal had been, and the camera pans to the open window, with the curtains blowing in the breeze, revealing that the criminal had escaped. William's orchestral music was driving the audience to discover where he had gone, but Hitchcock said, "You know, if you stop the music when the camera pans to the window, the silence will tell us that it's empty — he's gone, more emphatically, more powerfully than any musical phrase." Williams says it was a wonderful lesson where to arrange music in a film.

Directors today have a lot more control due to technology. Also, spotting decisions are very significant, but they can only go so far. Directors now have much more authorial control over the music than in Hitchcock's day because music sequencing software allows composers to closely replicate the final result, email this mock-up as an MP3 to the director until it is approved, and finally record it once completely approved.

The music in Tom Ford's film *A Single Man* (2009) is very Hitchcockian, beginning with urgent strings and an underwater dream sequence of a floating naked body. Ford wanted "a sort of overblown, Bernard Herrmannesque score...I had such great luck with a Russian composer called Abel Korzeniowski. I started off contacting Shigeru Umebayashi, who did *In the Mood for Love*, but he was not free to do the entire film. So he wrote a few small pieces. He sat in my office in L.A. and watched the movie for three days, and went back and wrote some very beautiful pieces of music...I had a very specific sound that I wanted. I wanted the principal instrument to be the violin, because the violin is the most human of all instruments. It can be sad and sound like it's crying. I think that the two scores mesh beautifully, and I don't think that you can tell where one ends and the other begins. Abel's great strength is his ability to score. Shigeru produces beautiful freestanding pieces, but Abel scores — he writes music to reinforce the moment."

Hitchcock's use of music later liberated the musical impulses of directors such as Martin Scorsese and Quentin Tarantino, who would frequently use music rather than dialogue to compelling effect. Think of Scorsese's use of "Jumping Jack Flash" as Robert De Niro waltzes through a bar in *Mean Streets* (1973), or Tarantino using "Stuck in the Middle With You" in *Reservoir Dogs* (1992).

EXERCISES

1. Watch *Psycho* with the sound turned off. Does it have the same impact? What feelings does it convey?

2. How does sound contribute to your story? To make your film more compelling, record and include ambient or natural sounds that illustrate the scene more than visuals alone can convey.

3. Experiment with silence in a sequence of your movie. How does it increase the atmosphere or tension?

4. Turn off the sound in *Rear Window* and then see if you can still understand the story from only the visuals.

5. Write down where your film could most benefit from music. What is the mood you are trying to convey and what is the most appropriate choice of music?

6. List sounds if you were filming in a train station.

Key Hitchcock films to watch

Blackmail (1926)
Rear Window (1954)
The Man Who Knew Too Much (1956)
Psycho (1960)
The Birds (1963)
Frenzy (1972)

Other directors' films to watch

Jaws (1975)
Signs (2002)
The Ghost Writer (2010)

Further reading

Film Music: A Very Short Introduction (2010) by Kathryn Marie Kalinak
Hitchcock's Music (2006) by Jack Sullivan
A Heart at Fire's Center: The Life and Music of Bernard Herrmann (1992) by Steven C. Smith

CHAPTER EIGHT

DON'T WORRY — IT'S ONLY A MOVIE

"A good film is when the price of the dinner, the theatre admission, and the babysitter were worth it. " — Alfred Hitchcock

You've made your movie, you've edited it, lovingly crafted it, added the music and the effects. Now you have to market it and get your film out there. Every director must know how to sell his films if he is to be successful in today's highly competitive industry, and developing your marketing skills is more critical than ever. Hitchcock knew this all too well and he was the master not only of suspense, but also of marketing. His cameo appearances and witty trailers became trademarks, all designed to sell the Hitchcock brand.

Early in his career Hitchcock set up his own public relations company, controlling all media coverage of his persona. By giving interviews, through tireless public-ity campaigns, gimmicks and stunts, he ensured that his name and his films were constantly in the public eye. He had the well-deserved reputation as the "Master of Suspense" because he was also a master of branding, and he managed to combine his artistic aspirations with his commercial interests when marketing his movies.

By the 1950s, Hitchcock had become the world's most recognizable film director, helped by the cameo appearances in his own films and by his tireless self-promotion. Hitchcock's name on a poster became a stamp of craftsmanship and a guarantee for a cinema experience of suspense, thrills, and mystery. He had a few cardinal rules for success along the way.

KNOW YOUR AUDIENCE

"I don't make pictures to please me. I make them to please audiences. " — Alfred Hitchcock

Hitchcock always tried to anticipate what the audience's reaction would be. When watching every scene in your movie, ask yourself, "What is the audience thinking now?" This is something that Hitchcock would do when working with his scriptwriter, and he recounted a remark that a play is not written or complete without an audience. You can have a play, you can rehearse it, and you can have a complete run-through. But until an audience witnesses that play, it is incomplete. The same principle applies to a film. In other words, there's no satisfaction in having a movie theater with only one seat filled. It's the audience and their reaction that gives interest to your movie.

"I think the most gratifying thing about this job is being able to appeal to world audiences," said Hitchcock. Film in its purest form is so vast because it can go all over the whole world. On any given night, your movie could be playing in Tokyo, Berlin, London, New York, and the different audiences all over the world are responding emotionally to the same things that they see on the screen — whether it's the story, the plot, the acting, or the dialogue. That's the power of the cinema. Theatre and literature doesn't have the same effect. But we are able, by the distributing films and placing them in movie houses throughout the world, to do that.

As an Englishman living in America, Hitchcock was fully aware that it was a country full of foreigners. He was very audience-conscious because he was appealing to many different types of people. Hitchcock also knew that 60% of the audience was female, and he catered to that audience too. When preparing *North by Northwest*, he famously said to Eva Marie Saint, "No more kitchen sink for you, Eva!" referring to her realist dramas like *On the Waterfront* (1954). Hitchcock was well ahead of the female liberation movement, always creating female characters who were independent, assertive, and sexually adventurous. (He was also aware that it's generally the woman who has the final say on which movie a couple goes to see.)

PROMOTE YOUR FILM

> *"Hitchcock has a distinctive style of his own. He is undoubtedly one of the few filmmakers on the horizon today whose screen signature can be identified as soon as the picture begins."*
> — *François Truffaut*

Some films succeed by chance. Word of mouth about a good film also attracts audiences and gets people talking. Hitchcock's promotion of *Psycho* is a master class of audience manipulation through promotion, gimmicks, and advertising. *Psycho* is one of the earliest examples of an independently financed ("indie") movie. Paramount wouldn't fund it and denied Hitchcock a proper budget, so the director went solo and funded the film through his own company, Shamley Productions. *Psycho* was made for

$800,000 and grossed more than $11 million in its first run alone, a huge amount of money for the time. Hitchcock owned every penny of *Psycho*, as he had invested his own money and the production belonged to him.

Hitchcock carefully controlled the promotion of the film. The stars didn't make the usual round of press junkets in the media; critics weren't given private screenings and Hitchcock created buzz for the film when he instigated a firm "no late admission" policy after the film had started. When *Psycho* was released, Hitchcock announced that nobody was to be admitted into the theatre after the film had started. This is because he wanted audiences to sit through the film from the beginning — and he didn't want them to give away the ending to their friends. This gimmick built a mystique around the film, and added to the suspense audiences already felt about attending.

Promotional material for *Psycho* stressed the strict ban on late admission. In print and on screen, Hitchcock often talked directly to his audience: "Surely you do not have your meat course after your dessert at dinner. You will therefore understand why we are so insistent that you enjoy *Psycho* from start to finish, exactly as we intended that it be served...[and] we said no one — not even the manager's brother, the President of the United States, or the Queen of England (God bless her)."

The audience had been sold this concept and with it they were sold *Psycho*. The campaign began with newspaper teaser ads, which explained and sold the policy and the "keep the story a secret" idea supplemented the policy. "A demonstration of revolutionary showmanship," described George Weltner, Vice President of Paramount Pictures World Sales. After refusing to finance *Psycho*, Paramount agreed to distribute it. Showings of the film began on a tightly controlled schedule in theatres in New York, Chicago, Boston, and Philadelphia, and it became one of the biggest grossers in Paramount Pictures history.

Martin Scorsese remembers the hysteria around *Psycho* when it was first released and coming out of the theatre and people shouting "What happened? What happened?" referring to the film's ending. He described the atmosphere generated as being like a carnival. Hitch's feeling about the movie was that up to the last moment you had to believe that Mrs. Bates was alive and that Norman Bates was innocent. Hitchcock even sent out a casting call for Mrs. Bates, and allowed no visitors on the set so that the secret could be maintained.

CULTIVATE A PERSONA

> *"Actors come and go, but the name of the director should stay clearly in the mind of the audiences. "* — *Alfred Hitchcock*

What does David Fincher look like? Or Wes Anderson? Or Christopher Nolan? You may have a hard time picking any of these directors out in publicity photographs. If you asked the man on the street to name a director, the only one many could think of would be Alfred Hitchcock. Indeed, if you lived in the U.S. during the 1950s and 1960s, you were sure to know what Alfred Hitchcock looked and sounded like. This was largely because of his television series *Alfred Hitchcock Presents* and *The Alfred Hitchcock Hour*, which together ran for nine years, from 1955 to 1964. Hitchcock delivered witty and lugubrious introductions to each episode, scripted for him by his trusted writer James Allardice. As Hitchcock said, "When he came to see me and said 'what sort of introductions do you want me to write for you?' I said 'well, I won't tell you, but I'll run the film for you.' So I ran *The Trouble With Harry*. That's the kind of thing, you follow that route."

With these wittily macabre introductions, Hitchcock cleverly cultivated his persona and physique as a major promotional tool for his films, making fun of his famous

 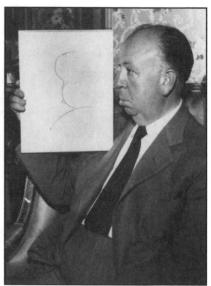

Hitchcock draws his famous signature profile.

profile, pudgy face, and portly frame. As big as the stars were in his films, it was his name alone that went above the title. The audience wanted to see a Hitchcock film partly because they knew what to expect from him — wit, sophistication, and suspense. His trademark silhouette profile became an instantly recognizable logo and is still being used in branding on DVDs and Blu-rays.

HAVE YOUR OWN SIGNATURE

"Brand products are always better products. Ask for them by name." — Alfred Hitchcock

Hitchcock boldly displayed his signature across the titles of his very first film as director of *The Pleasure Garden* (1925). Later he devised a simple nine-stroke caricature of himself in profile, which made him the only director in film history to have his own personal logo. He famously sketched this caricature during interviews, and for fans, to promote himself and his films. He was also one of the few directors to have his name above the title, which started in 1942 with *Alfred Hitchcock's Saboteur*. It's personal branding at its best.

As well as a signature, thanks to his television series Hitchcock had his own musical theme — Charles Gounod's *Funeral March of a Marionette,* a classical piece that most likely more people now associate with Hitchcock than Gounod.

DON'T WORRY ABOUT BEING PIGEON-HOLED

> *"I am a typed director. If I made* Cinderella, *the audience would immediately be looking for a body in the coach. "* — *Alfred Hitchcock*

Unlike other directors, almost all of Hitchcock's films fall into the same genre category — suspense. By sticking to a certain type of filmmaking, Hitchcock became closely associated with the suspense thriller, and soon became top of his craft. Hitchcock knew early on that he had this movie genre all to himself, because he had a true understanding of the film medium, while other directors didn't have such a firm grasp. During the time he was making these movies, he was able to hone his skill at building suspense. By specializing, Hitchcock was able to link his name with his craft, so that when a moviegoer was in the mood for a suspense film, he would go to a Hitchcock film and knew what to expect.

Yet despite specializing in thrillers and suspense, Hitchcock showed a remarkable range and diversity. "I do not believe it is necessary for a director to change his style in order to develop new characters and a different story in each film," Hitchcock said. "Style in directing develops slowly and naturally, as it does in everything else. I began to get more and more interested in developing a suspense technique."

Hitchcock managed to make movies that showed remarkable range and subject matter. Just think of some of his most popular films: *Rebecca*, *Rear Window*, *Psycho*, *Vertigo*, *Strangers on a Train*, *The Birds*, *Lifeboat*, *Shadow of a Doubt*, *Spellbound*, *To Catch a Thief*, *The Trouble With Harry*, *Frenzy*, *Notorious*. While all being suspenseful films in some way, they are strikingly different in tone and content.

SURROUND YOURSELF WITH TALENT

Hitchcock was a master technician who surrounded himself with top-notch talent — cinematographer Robert Burks, editor George Tomasini, art designer Robert Boyle, composer Bernard Herrmann, costume designer Edith Head — each of them was an expert in their craft. If you want to be the best, surround yourself with good people. As Gilbert Taylor, Hitch's DP on *Frenzy*, said. "Hitchcock used professionals and allowed them freedom to do their job, instead of pretending to know it all."

He also chose actors who were both major stars and major talents, whom he knew he could rely on to deliver. Cary Grant, Grace Kelly, James Stewart, Henry Fonda, Ingrid Bergman, Gregory Peck all exuded both star quality and dramatic ability. And Hitch surrounded these stars with the finest supporting players, many of whom he called upon again and again.

BE THE BEST SALESMAN FOR YOUR FILMS

When it comes to publicizing your film, a director is not that much different than a traveling salesman. You need to be prepared to go to movie junkets, festivals, do interviews, and have tireless energy. Hitchcock worked tirelessly to promote his films with promotional tours and knew that they were very important to the success of the film and had to be timed just right.

"He was the first director as *star*" says Scott Hicks, the director of *Shine* (1996). Director Eli Roth says, "One thing that I love about Hitchcock was that he was really the first director that put his personality before the movie. I mean, it was Alfred Hitchcock's *North by Northwest*, even though Ernest Lehman, of course, wrote it, and, of course, there was a novel and the script of *Psycho*, but it's Alfred Hitchcock's *Psycho*. You really feel his personality in all of the movies."

HAVE A MEMORABLE MOVIE TITLE

Hitchcock's films echo with snappy movie titles, often one word, such as *Spellbound*, *Notorious*, *Vertigo*, *Psycho*, and *Frenzy*. In fact, 18 of Hitchcock's films have one-word titles. Hitchcock believed that an efficient title gave a film focus during production, and that a good title is its own trailer. The best titles offer a sense of mystery while summarizing the meaning of a film without giving anything away.

Titles can have mystery and suspense, such as *The 39 Steps*, *Strangers on a Train*, *The Man Who Knew Too Much*, and *North by Northwest*. Instantly you want to know what the film is about because of the intriguing title.

A great recent film title was the Samuel L. Jackson thriller *Snakes on a Plane*. Like Hitchcock's *The Birds* and *Psycho*, the title says it all. In each case the audience is clear what the film is about, and is excited at the thought of encountering what the title promises.

With the advent of social media and social networks such as Facebook and Twitter, low-budget films with great titles can now easily become Internet sensations, generating endless free publicity. Made for a mere $15,000, *Paranormal Activity* grossed more than $193 million at the box office. What did it have? Intriguing online teasers — and a great title!

TAGLINES AND POSTERS

A catchy tagline can help sell your movie, pique curiosity, and encourage audiences to come and see it. Hitchcock himself had a hand in fashioning the taglines of his films. Here are a few:

> *Saboteur* — "Unmasking the man behind your back!"

> *The Man Who Knew Too Much* — "A little knowledge can be a deadly thing!"

> *The Birds* — "The next scream you hear may be your own!"

> *Torn Curtain* — "It will tear you apart with suspense!"

A tagline should define the tone of your film in a single line, identifying its genre while at the same time conveying a hint of storyline to the potential viewer.

For *The Birds*, Hitchcock came up with the clever tagline "The Birds is Coming!" which was used as the slogan on the advertising posters, as well car bumper stickers. Of course the line is grammatically incorrect, but it's memorable and fun.

Linked to the tagline is a good poster, which can help boost sales and generate buzz about a film. Hitchcock's poster for the re-release of *Rear Window* cleverly back-referenced Psycho — "See it! If your nerves can stand it after *Psycho*!"

TRAILERS

Hitchcock often appeared in his own movie trailers, urging filmgoers to see his new film, and sometimes even masterminded the publicity campaigns. We can see Hitchcock's mastery of the moviemaking business by looking at the trailers he designed for his films. From his first film in America, *Rebecca* (1940), the trailer played up the fact that it was an Alfred Hitchcock film, as well as a David O.

Selznick production, and that it was "The most glamorous film of all time!"

Hitchcock's trailers for the most part were witty and inventive. One of his best is "A Guided Tour with Alfred Hitchcock" for *North by Northwest*, where Hitch helps the viewer plan a summer vacation — very apt for a movie that takes us all over the U.S. map.

Director David Fincher makes it a point to be involved heavily in the trailer process, but some filmmakers aren't well versed enough in what sells and why. The real point is to be disarming while still advocating your work. With the huge impact of the Internet, one of the best modern directors using this medium to promote their films is Peter Jackson with his extensive video blogs of his productions. He's grabbing the spotlight, letting fans in on the process and delivering the goods even before the movie has begun shooting. That's good salesmanship.

THE CAMEO

"My cameo appearances were reminding the audience, it's only a movie." — Alfred Hitchcock

Alfred Hitchcock was among the first directors to have a cameo appearance in his films. He started appearing in his own films early in his directing career simply because extras were needed to fill crowd scenes. It started with *The Lodger* (1927) in a newspaper scene — "I'm seen seated foreground at a desk, because in a scene of that kind, we didn't bother to engage actors," says Hitch. His first big cameo was in *Blackmail* (1929), where he appeared in a subway scene. That got journalists talking and *The New York Times* magazine soon ran a list of where he appeared in the cameos.

After that Hitchcock appeared in all his films and his cameos became much loved. He appeared in front of the camera in more than 30 of his films, where he would often poke a little fun of himself. His portly figure was often used to humorous effect. He added the cameos to get audiences and critics talking. These fleeting, inventive and humorous appearances became a trademark, and audiences delighted in catching a glimpse of him.

As Hitchcock became more and more famous, particularly thanks to his weekly introductions for the television series *Alfred Hitchcock Presents* and *The Alfred Hitchcock Hour*, he worried that audiences would spend too much time watching out for him, and not enough on the plot. So his cameo appearances appeared early in each film, so that once the audience had spotted him, they could get on with the movie itself.

Lifeboat — A dieting advertisement in a newspaper.

Strangers on a Train — Getting on a train with a double bass.

Rear Window — Winding up a clock in one of the apartment windows.

North by Northwest — Attempting to catch a bus.

Hitchcock misses the bus at the beginning of *North by Northwest* (1959).

Hitchcock's cameo in *The Birds* (1963), with Tippi Hedren and Hitch's own dogs Geoffrey and Stanley.

The Birds — Leaving a pet shop, accompanied by his beloved Sealyham terriers Geoffrey and Stanley.

Family Plot — Behind the door of the registrar of births and deaths (probably reporting a death).

CAMEO APPEARANCES BY OTHER DIRECTORS

"I have wormed my way into my own pictures as a spy. A director should see how the other half lives." — Alfred Hitchcock

Other directors have followed in Hitchcock's footsteps with cameo appearances, including Peter Jackson, Eli Roth, and Sam Raimi, while others sometimes give themselves larger parts in their own movies, such as Quentin Tarantino and Kevin Smith. Raimi has always been a fan of Hitchcock. "I love how funny he is. He must have been the funniest actor in Hollywood in the late '50s and early '60s. When I see his cameos and his most incredibly, hysterically droll performances in *Alfred Hitchcock Presents*, there's nobody I can think of who would have been funnier."

Some directors have gone for more prominent cameos, such as Francis Ford Coppola's TV director in *Apocalypse Now* (1979), Oliver Stone's trader in the split-screen sequence in *Wall Street* (1987), or Martin Scorsese's photographer in *Hugo* (2011). M. Night Shyamalan, director of *The Sixth Sense* (1999) and *Signs* (2002), seeks a more active role, actually casting himself in small parts in his movies. He says, "It's important for me to be a part of the film in some way rather than to be an outsider from the independent world of filmmaking. I would love to play the lead role, but it's physically impossible."

John Carpenter and Peter Jackson have tended to follow Hitchcock's lead in combining ubiquity with anonymity. In *The Lovely Bones* (2009), look out for Peter Jackson's cameo in the scenes inside the mall, where you'll catch the director posing as a shopper examining an old-fashion video camera. "It was weird," he explained. "The film is set in 1973, and I was 12 years old at that particular time. And when I was 12, I was making home movies with my camera and dreaming of becoming a filmmaker. We had this wonderful shopping mall that we put all these 1973 props around, and there was a photo store and they had a Super 8 camera that was exactly the same camera that I used when I was 12 years old! So it seemed like a natural cameo for me to be someone in the store looking at the Super 8 camera." Jackson says audiences chuckled when they saw his cameo, even though he was being serious. The point is that it gets audiences talking about both the film and the filmmaker.

Eli Roth says, "I've always tried to do a little walk-on cameo in my films, in all my films, because of Hitchcock. That's why every director does a cameo in their movies, because Hitchcock did it." Director Guillermo del Toro shares his love of Hitchcock's movies, and also shares the director's portly physique. "I learned to love my strangeness, that's what I learned from Hitchcock. Both of us have sort of outsider points of view — I don't think that he was ever fully integrated into society — we're always a little bit of the anarchist, fat, funny guy." So use your physique!

GOING FOR GIMMICKS

Hitchcock was the master of gimmicks. He devised elaborate marketing campaigns for his films, especially *North by Northwest*, *Psycho*, and *The Birds*. The gimmicks gained extra public attention and added an element of fun. During the promotion of *The Birds*, he had many gimmicks during the movie's screening, such as a pair of lovebirds named Alfie and Tippi. And during the premiere of the film at the Cannes Film Festival, Hitchcock and Hedren released a flock of pigeons into the sky.

The "no late admittance" rule for *Psycho* was a gimmick designed to generate interest. There was similar buzz around a later film with a plot twist that audiences were urged to keep a secret — *The Crying Game* (1992). For *The Blair Witch Project* (1999), an Internet campaign suggested that the movie was real. The film grossed $250 million worldwide, with a filming budget of less than $25,000, making it one of the most successful independent movies of all time. As Arthur Hiller, the director of *Love Story* (who also directed for *Alfred Hitchcock Presents*) says, "His work taught me not to be afraid, to be adventuresome, and the necessity of surprising the audience with an innovative twist or unusual turn, unfamiliar

Hitchcock shares a photo op with cast members. (*The Birds*, 1963)

yet believable, that takes the audience away from the path you had been taking them on."

One way to get people talking about your movie is to push the envelope with innovation and censorship. Hitchcock loved to push things a little further with the censors. It was sort of a game with him and Geoffrey Shurlock, the head of the Hays Code, which regulated movies. Hitch knew that word-of-mouth publicity was invaluable and that it could be achieved through things such as sex and violence and suggestive dialogue. He fought censorship battles over homosexual overtones in *Rope*, risqué dialogue in *Rear Window* and *North by Northwest*, and even the sound of a toilet flushing in *Psycho*. And of course, he spun these battles into publicity. Hitchcock knew that word of mouth about these hot topics would get the audience talking — and talk was good.

EXERCISES

1. Think of films where the opening titles suggest the mood of a picture. What do they say about the films?

2. What is your movie about? Try to write a one-line tagline for it. Is it catchy? Memorable? Would your friend want to go and see the movie from reading the tagline? Look at the movie listings in *TV Guide* for examples of well-conceived loglines.

3. Write down a list of popular movie genres; suspense, horror, adventure, western, romantic comedy. What appeals to you most? What kind of movie director do you want to be?

4. Take a recent example of a successful movie and show how it's marketed. How does it make use of social media, the Internet, and trailers to generate word of mouth?

Hitchcock films to watch

Psycho (1960)
The Birds (1963)
Family Plot (1976)

Other directors' films to watch

Cape Fear (1991)
Basic Instinct (1992)
Mulholland Dr. (2001)
The Silence of the Lambs (1991)
Memento (2001)

Further reading

Alfred Hitchcock and the Making of Psycho (1998) by Stephen Rebello
Hitchcock: The Making of a Reputation (1992) by Robert Kapsis

CONCLUSION

"I think that students should be taught to visualize. That's the one thing missing in all this. The one thing that the student has got to do is learn that there is a rectangle up there — a white rectangle in a theatre — and it has to be filled." — Alfred Hitchcock

Congratulations, you have reached the end of the master class. But don't rest on your laurels here. This should be only the beginning, as this book is intended as a continuing resource for film students and aspiring directors. There's always something new and exciting to discover from Hitchcock's films through repeated viewings — you'll be guaranteed to spot something that you missed the last time. I recommend that you watch Hitchcock's films to develop your own style. Know your audience and what makes them laugh or scream. Become a complete filmmaker with a broad understanding of storytelling, scriptwriting, costuming, storyboarding, directing, scoring, and editing. Take time to learn your craft and revel in what you do.

Use the principles outlined in this master class to make a good movie great. Hitchcock was able to combine the right mix of suspense, romance, humor, and the sheer power of storytelling.

Most of all, enjoy what you do. Relax. As Hitchcock said, "Don't worry, it's only a movie!"

ALFRED HITCHCOCK FILMOGRAPHY

The Pleasure Garden (1925)

The Mountain Eagle (1926)

The Lodger (1927)

The Ring (1927)

Downhill (1927)

The Farmer's Wife (1928)

Easy Virtue (1928)

Champagne (1928)

The Manxman (1929)

Blackmail (1929)

Juno and the Paycock (1930)

Murder! (1930)

Elstree Calling (1930)

The Skin Game (1931)

Mary (1931)

Rich and Strange (1931)

Number Seventeen (1932)

Waltzes from Vienna (1933)

The Man Who Knew Too Much (1934)

The 39 Steps (1935)

Secret Agent (1936)

Sabotage (1936)

Young and Innocent (1937)

The Lady Vanishes (1938)

Jamaica Inn (1939)

Rebecca (1940)

Foreign Correspondent (1940)

Mr. & Mrs. Smith (1941)

Suspicion (1941)

Saboteur (1942)

Shadow of a Doubt (1943)

Lifeboat (1944)

Bon Voyage (1944)

Spellbound (1945)

Notorious (1946)

The Paradine Case (1947)

Rope (1948)

Under Capricorn (1949)

Stage Fright (1950)

Strangers on a Train (1951)

I Confess (1953)

Dial M for Murder (1954)

Rear Window (1954)

To Catch a Thief (1955)

The Trouble With Harry (1955)

The Man Who Knew Too Much (1956)

The Wrong Man (1956)

Vertigo (1958)

North by Northwest (1959)

Psycho (1960)

The Birds (1963)

Marnie (1964)

Torn Curtain (1966)

Topaz (1969)

Frenzy (1972)

Family Plot (1976)

LIST OF DIRECTORS INFLUENCED BY HITCHCOCK

Abrams, J.J. (*Lost, Super 8*)

Almodóvar, Pedro (*Bad Education, Broken Embraces, The Skin I Live In*)

Amenábar, Alejandro (*The Others, Open Your Eyes*)

Benton, Robert (*The Late Show, Still of the Night*)

Burton, Tim (*Ed Wood*)

Carnahan, Joe (*Narc, The A-Team*)

Carpenter, John (*Halloween*)

Caruso, D.J. (*Disturbia*)

Craven, Wes (*Scream, Red Eye*)

Del Toro, Guillermo (*Pan's Labyrinth*)

Demme, Jonathan (*The Silence of the Lambs*)

DePalma, Brian (*Carrie, Dressed to Kill, Obsession, Femme Fatal*)

Fincher, David (*Seven, Panic Room*)

Ford, Tom (*A Single Man*)

Friedkin, William (*The Exorcist, To Live and Die in L.A.*)

Greengrass, Paul (*United 93, The Bourne Supremacy, Bloody Sunday*)

Haneke, Michael (*Caché*)

Hanson, Curtis (*The Bedroom Window, L.A. Confidential*)

Holland, Tom (*Fright Night, Child's Play*)

Jackson, Peter (*King Kong, The Lovely Bones*)

Jones, Duncan (*Source Code*)

Lucas, George (*Star Wars*)

Lynch, David (*Blue Velvet, Twin Peaks, Mulholland Dr.*)

Minghella, Anthony (*The Talented Mr. Ripley*)

Nolan, Christopher (*Memento, Insomnia, Inception*)

Nolfi, George (*The Bourne Ultimatum, The Adjustment Bureau*)

Noyce, Phillip (*Dead Calm, The Bone Collector*)

Parker, Alan (*Angel Heart, Mississippi Burning*)

Polanski, Roman (*Macbeth, The Ghost Writer*)

Raimi, Sam (*The Quick and the Dead, Spider-Man*)

Roth, Eli (*Hostel, Cabin*)

Sanchez, Eduardo and Myrick, Daniel (*The Blair Witch Project*)

Scorsese, Martin (*Taxi Driver, Raging Bull, Cape Fear, Shutter Island*)

Schlesinger, John (*Midnight Cowboy, Cold Comfort Farm*)

Schumacher, Joel (*Phone Booth*)

Shyamalan, M. Night (*The Sixth Sense, Unbreakable, Signs, The Village*)

Singer, Bryan (*The Usual Suspects*)

Soderbergh, Steven (*Ocean's Eleven, Contagion*)

Spielberg, Steven (*Jaws, Raiders of the Lost Ark, Munich*)

Tarantino, Quentin (*Reservoir Dogs, Pulp Fiction, Inglourious Basterds*)

Verhoeven, Paul (*The Fourth Man, Basic Instinct*)

Von Trier, Lars (*Dogville*)

Woo, John (*Hard Boiled, Mission: Impossible 2, Paycheck*)

BIBLIOGRAPHY & REFERENCES

Books

Aulier, Dan (1998) *Vertigo: The Making of a Hitchcock Classic*

Bogdanovich, Peter (1997) *Who the Devil Made It?*

Gottlieb, Sidney (1997) *Hitchcock on Hitchcock*

Gottlieb, Sidney (2003) *Alfred Hitchcock: Interviews (Conversations with Filmmakers)*

Krohn, Bill (2000) *Hitchcock at Work*

McGilligan, Patrick (2003) *Alfred Hitchcock: A Life in Darkness and Light*

Moral, Tony Lee (2013) *Hitchcock and the Making of Marnie, 2nd edition*

Moral, Tony Lee (2013) *The Making of Hitchcock's The Birds*

Truffaut, François (1967) *Hitchcock*

Rebello, Stephen (1990) *Alfred Hitchcock and the Making of Psycho*

Wood, Robin (1989) *Hitchcock's Films Revisited*

Hitchcock lectures

1939 lecture at Radio City Music Hall, New York City

1963 interview with Peter Bogdanovich

1966 lecture at Harvard University

1972 lecture at the American Film Institute

ABOUT THE AUTHOR

Tony Lee Moral has been interested in Hitchcock's films ever since he saw *I Confess* at an early age. He took part in the 1999 Hitchcock centenary in New York and met many of Hitchcock's collaborators. His first book *Hitchcock and the Making of Marnie* was published in the U.S. by Rowman & Littlefield in 2002 and in the UK by Manchester University Press, and his second book *The Making of Hitchcock's The Birds* was published by Kamera Books.

His appreciation of Hitchcock's films deepens with every viewing as there is something new to discover and learn from the "Master." He has produced and directed more than 100 hours of television for American and British broadcasting channels, filming all over the world.

Tony's favorite Hitchcock films are *Notorious*, *Rear Window*, *Vertigo*, *North by Northwest*, *Psycho*, *The Birds*, and *Marnie*. He is still searching for the elusive MacGuffin.

He spends his time between London and Los Angeles.

www.tonyleemoral.com
www.alfredhitchcockbooks.com

"What's my idea of happiness? A clear horizon, nothing to worry about on your plate, only things that are creative and not destructive. **"**
— Alfred Hitchcock

SAVE THE CAT!®
THE LAST BOOK ON SCREENWRITING YOU'LL EVER NEED!

BLAKE SNYDER

BEST SELLER

He's made millions of dollars selling screenplays to Hollywood and now screenwriter Blake Snyder tells all. "Save the Cat!." is just one of Snyder's many ironclad rules for making your ideas more marketable and your script more satisfying — and saleable, including:
- The four elements of every winning logline.
- The seven immutable laws of screenplay physics.
- The 10 genres and why they're important to your movie.
- Why your Hero must serve your idea.
- Mastering the Beats.
- Mastering the Board to create the Perfect Beast.
- How to get back on track with ironclad and proven rules for script repair.

This ultimate insider's guide reveals the secrets that none dare admit, told by a show biz veteran who's proven that you can sell your script if you can save the cat.

"Imagine what would happen in a town where more writers approached screenwriting the way Blake suggests? My weekend read would dramatically improve, both in sellable/producible content and in discovering new writers who understand the craft of storytelling and can be hired on assignment for ideas we already have in house."
> – From the Foreword by Sheila Hanahan Taylor, Vice President, Development at Zide/Perry Entertainment, whose films include *American Pie, Cats and Dogs, Final Destination*

"One of the most comprehensive and insightful how-to's out there. Save the Cat!. is a must-read for both the novice and the professional screenwriter."
> – Todd Black, Producer, *The Pursuit of Happyness, The Weather Man, S.W.A.T, Alex and Emma, Antwone Fisher*

"Want to know how to be a successful writer in Hollywood? The answers are here. Blake Snyder has written an insider's book that's informative — and funny, too."
> – David Hoberman, Producer, *The Shaggy Dog* (2005), *Raising Helen, Walking Tall, Bringing Down the House, Monk* (TV)

BLAKE SNYDER, besides selling million-dollar scripts to both Disney and Spielberg, was one of Hollywood's most successful spec screenwriters. Blake's vision continues on *www.blakesnyder.com.*

$19.95 · 216 PAGES · ORDER NUMBER 34RLS · ISBN: 9781932907001

24 HOURS | 1.800.833.5738 | WWW.MWP.COM

THE WRITER'S JOURNEY
3RD EDITION

MYTHIC STRUCTURE FOR WRITERS

CHRISTOPHER VOGLER

BEST SELLER
OVER 170,000 COPIES SOLD!

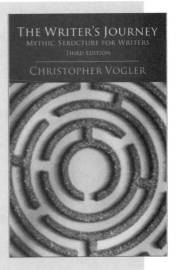

See why this book has become an international best seller and a true classic. *The Writer's Journey* explores the powerful relationship between mythology and storytelling in a clear, concise style that's made it required reading for movie executives, screenwriters, playwrights, scholars, and fans of pop culture all over the world.

Both fiction and nonfiction writers will discover a set of useful myth-inspired storytelling paradigms (i.e., "The Hero's Journey") and step-by-step guidelines to plot and character development. Based on the work of Joseph Campbell, *The Writer's Journey* is a must for all writers interested in further developing their craft.

The updated and revised third edition provides new insights and observations from Vogler's ongoing work on mythology's influence on stories, movies, and man himself.

"This book is like having the smartest person in the story meeting come home with you and whisper what to do in your ear as you write a screenplay. Insight for insight, step for step, Chris Vogler takes us through the process of connecting theme to story and making a script come alive."
> – Lynda Obst, Producer, *Sleepless in Seattle, How to Lose a Guy in 10 Days;* Author, *Hello, He Lied*

"This is a book about the stories we write, and perhaps more importantly, the stories we live. It is the most influential work I have yet encountered on the art, nature, and the very purpose of storytelling."
> – Bruce Joel Rubin, Screenwriter, *Stuart Little 2, Deep Impact, Ghost, Jacob's Ladder*

CHRISTOPHER VOGLER is a veteran story consultant for major Hollywood film companies and a respected teacher of filmmakers and writers around the globe. He has influenced the stories of movies from *The Lion King* to *Fight Club* to *The Thin Red Line* and most recently wrote the first installment of *Ravenskull*, a Japanese-style manga or graphic novel. He is the executive producer of the feature film *P.S. Your Cat is Dead* and writer of the animated feature *Jester Till*.

$26.95 · 300 PAGES · ORDER NUMBER 76RLS · ISBN: 193290736x

24 HOURS | **1.800.833.5738** | **WWW.MWP.COM**

DAN O'BANNON'S GUIDE TO SCREENPLAY STRUCTURE

INSIDE TIPS FROM THE WRITER OF ALIEN, TOTAL RECALL & RETURN OF THE LIVING DEAD

DAN O'BANNON WITH MATT R. LOHR

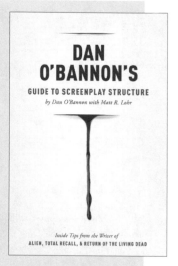

Dan O'Bannon (1946–2009), the acclaimed writer/director whose credits include *Alien*, *Total Recall*, and *Return of the Living Dead*, presents a masterful collection of the storytelling wisdom and insights that he used to create mega-hit classic motion pictures.

Dan O'Bannon famously crafted his screenplays using a self-designed system which he called "dynamic structure." This book outlines how O'Bannon's method differs from those of other well-known screenwriting gurus, and illustrates with examples from classic (and not-so-classic) films how dynamic structure can be applied to craft narrative and character. O'Bannon also includes his insights on subjects such as the logic of the three-act structure, the role of the producer in screenplay development, and the psychological principle known as "hedonic adaptation," which has a unique effect on the structuring of screen stories.

"Written in a style that carefully blends the personal and the professional, Dan O'Bannon's Guide to Screenplay Structure is more than a book. It is like an opportunity to sit down with a Hollywood insider over coffee and get the skinny on what it takes to make it in the business."

— Dr. Gregory K. Allen, supervising professor, The Sprocket Guild

"A successful screenwriter, Dan O'Bannon is more invested in great writing than in obeying rules. At the core of his book are twelve case studies of classic plays and scripts. The book analyzes each work with O'Bannon's story structural system. It shows you how the rules apply and, perhaps equally important, when they don't and why. You can use the book as a workbook, a guide, or a call to excellence. This book can be useful for writers at any level and for scripts at any stage of development."

— Mildred Lewis, award-winning filmmaker and playwright;
cofounder, The Fox Lewis Project

DAN O'BANNON was an acclaimed screenwriter whose eleven feature writing credits include the international blockbusters *Alien* and *Total Recall*, as well as *Return of the Living Dead*, which he also directed.

MATT R. LOHR is an award-winning screenwriter, essayist, and critic. His views on contemporary and classic cinema can be found on his blog, "The Movie Zombie." He lives in Los Angeles.

$26.95 · 264 PAGES · ORDER NUMBER 188RLS · ISBN: 9781615931309

In a dark time, a light bringer came along, leading the curious and the frustrated to clarity and empowerment. It took the well-guarded secrets out of the hands of the few and made them available to all. It spread a spirit of openness and creative freedom, and built a storehouse of knowledge dedicated to the betterment of the arts.

The essence of the Michael Wiese Productions (MWP) is empowering people who have the burning desire to express themselves creatively. We help them realize their dreams by putting the tools in their hands. We demystify the sometimes secretive worlds of screenwriting, directing, acting, producing, film financing, and other media crafts.

By doing so, we hope to bring forth a realization of 'conscious media' which we define as being positively charged, emphasizing hope and affirming positive values like trust, cooperation, self-empowerment, freedom, and love. Grounded in the deep roots of myth, it aims to be healing both for those who make the art and those who encounter it. It hopes to be transformative for people, opening doors to new possibilities and pulling back veils to reveal hidden worlds.

MWP has built a storehouse of knowledge unequaled in the world, for no other publisher has so many titles on the media arts. Please visit www.mwp.com where you will find many free resources and a 25% discount on our books. Sign up and become part of the wider creative community!

Onward and upward,

Michael Wiese
Publisher/Filmmaker